PAUL, THE LETTER WRITER

PAUL, THE LETTER WRITER

M. Luther Stirewalt, Jr.

WILLIAM B. EERDMANS PUBLISHING COMPANY
GRAND RAPIDS, MICHIGAN / CAMBRIDGE, U.K.

Wm. B. Eerdmans Publishing Co.
255 Jefferson Ave. S.E., Grand Rapids, Michigan 49503 /
P.O. Box 163, Cambridge CB3 9PU U.K.

Printed in the United States of America

08 07 06 05 04 03   7 6 5 4 3 2 1

Library of Congress Cataloging-in-Publication Data

Stirewalt, M. Luther, 1913-
Paul, the letter writer / M. Luther Stirewalt, Jr.
p.   cm.
Includes bibliographical references and index.
ISBN-10 0-8028-6088-5 / ISBN-13 978-0-8028-6088-0 (pbk.: alk. paper)
1. Bible. N.T. Epistles of Paul — Criticism, interpretation, etc.
2. Bible. N.T. Epistles of Paul — Language, style. 3. Greek letters —
History and criticism. 4. Letter writing, Greek. I. Title.
BS2650.52 S75 2003
227′.066 — dc21

2002033890

www.eerdmans.com

Contents

I

The Logistics of Ancient Greek Letter Writing

The term *logistics* refers to the means by which a letter is composed, delivered, and received. In Hellenic society there was a marked difference between the logistics of personal letter writing and official letter writing. It is the intention of this chapter to show that Paul fashioned the logistics for his communications after the examples offered by official correspondence. This observation serves as an introduction to his adaptation of official letter characteristics in his apostolic communications.

A. Epistolary Logistics in Secular Correspondence

1. The Personal Letter

Commoners could write their own letters, or they could employ a servant, a literate friend, or a public scribe to do so.[1] Most often preparing a letter was a solitary endeavor; few commoners had a secretary like Cicero's Tiro or an organized, supportive community like Paul's.[2] The

---

1. For the public scribe see, George Milligan, *Here and There among the Papyri* (London: Hodder & Stoughton, 1922), 38ff.; E. Randolf Richards, *The Secretary in the Letters of Paul*, WUNT 2:42 (Tübingen: Mohr/Siebeck, 1991), 20-23 and literature.

2. One may assume that writers such as Plato, Epicurus, the orators, and the writers of letter-essays had facilities for preparing, dispatching and/or publishing their letters other than the limited means available to other people. Greek households may also have had secretaries like Cicero's Tiro. For more on Tiro see Richards, *Secretary*, 44-47.

community aspect of a personal letter was limited to the involvement of, or reference to, family and friends for the exchange of greetings and the tending to whatever business was at hand.

There was no organized postal system for the common citizen; the dispatch of personal correspondence was largely a matter of chance and good fortune.[3] The trust and hope placed in the goodwill of strangers is concentrated in the simple, forthright directive on an out-side address from an early period: "Carry this to the pottery works and deliver it to Nausias or Thrasycles or his son."[4] Dionysius the Sophist wrote, "I've received one letter from you; this will be your fourth from me, if anyone delivers it to you."[5] Sending one of his or her own ser-vants as courier was the only way a sender could exercise any control over the delivery of a letter.[6] In one of Euripides' plays Iphigenia reads a letter aloud to the carrier so that, if the missive is somehow lost, he may deliver its message orally, and there is evidence that Roman fami-lies of means took turns supplying a slave to deliver letters to relatives in the provinces.[7] Needless to say, the more important the message the more trustworthy the bearer had to be.[8] A friend making a trip might be pressed into service,[9] or a professional carrier might be paid for the

---

3. For a detailed presentation of the extent of letter writing and the delivery of let-ters see Eldon J. Epp, "New Testament Papyrus Manuscripts and Letter Carrying in Greco-Roman Times," in *The Future of Early Christianity: Essays in Honor of Helmut Koester,* ed. Birger A. Pearson (Minneapolis: Fortress, 1991), 35-56; see especially 43-56. For a survey of delivery systems for official and private mail see John L. White, *Light from Ancient Letters* (Philadelphia: Fortress, 1986), 214-15; Richards, *Secretary,* 7-10. Rich-ards' definitive work is largely based on private letters (e.g. pp. 11, 169), and through-out he treats Paul's letters as belonging to that category. He recognizes his depen-dency on Cicero (p. 13 and note 69). He thinks in terms of forgery for fictitious letters (pp. 42-43, 16).

4. W. Crönert, "Die beiden ältesten griechischen Briefe," *Rein Mus* 65 (1910): 157-60. See nos. 14, 17, 27 in Chan-Hie Kim and John L. White, *Letters from the Papyri: A Study Collection,* Consultation on Ancient Epistolography, SBL Epistolography Seminar, 1974 (unpub-lished).

5. *Ep.* 29. See also from a recruit in Italy: Hunt and Edgar, LCL I 111; Plato *Ep.* 3 317; Chion *Ep.* 9.

6. E. *IT* 725ff.; see the discussion of the relation of a personal, incriminating message and a trusted carrier in Antiphon, *Or.* 5 52ff.

7. G. H. Stevenson, *OCD* s.v. "Tabellarii," p. 875.

8. Hdt. I 23; E. *IA.* 111-114; Chion *Ep.* 17; J. *Ant.* 18 182.

9. A family member *PSI* 1080, iii CE (Hunt and Edgar, LCL I 132); and Basil *Ep.* 19; or

task.[10] It is likely that sea captains, too, often carried letters.[11] These, though, were the opportunities of the fortunate; others were dependent on strangers and travelers whom they chanced to meet on the way, in the marketplace, or at the wharf.[12]

Perhaps there was no postal system because the private sector lacked a precedent for establishing and supporting such a public service, but also it should be ascribed to a distrust of the written word and to the nature of the personal letter as a substitute for oral speech. It was generally thought that one might better send an oral message to an absent friend through an intermediary who could then continue a conversation. Certainly complaints at having to resort to letter-writing were made.[13] The advantage and value of the letter itself was that it served as confirmation of the business at hand, and especially in the case of the familial letter, the writing material and the few phrases on it were sent "as a gift."[14]

The oral background of the personal letter is reflected in its reception.[15] To be sure, privacy and intimacy were recognized and respected. Seals were honored and conscientious and direct delivery was often possible. The delivery of a letter could be considered a sacred trust. Alexander the Great received personal letters from Olympia, his mother; once Hephaestion and Alexander read one of them together, and afterward Alexander touched his signet ring to his friend's lips.[16] The orator

---

a friend who happened to be making a trip might be pressed into service Isoc. *Ep.* 7; Soc. *Ep.* 21.

10. J. *Life* 224, see 297; Pliny III 17 (certainly in jest).

11. Arr. *Epict.* III 24 23-26; Them. *Ep.* 7 *init.*

12. Chion *Epp.* 2, 4; Them. *Ep.* 5; Diog. *Ep.* 6; see Diony. Soph. *Ep.* 29. It is assumed that in the fictitious letters the usual conditions prevailed and even added to the dramatic effect.

13. Isoc. *Ep.* I 1-2; see III 4; Diog. 17; 2 John 12; 3 John 13-14; and the special pleading for the effectiveness of a letter in Diog. *Ep.* 3.

14. Dem. *de Eloc.* 244. See *PMich* VIII 481 = no. 112 in White, *Light;* the carrier is also to deliver a basket and the sender wants an accounting of the contents; see also *PFay* CXXX; Soc. *Ep.* 21; Chion *Ep.* 6.

15. The oral message corroborated the written word (Isoc. *Ep.* 7 10; Basil *Ep.* 5 *init.;* Col 4:7-9). Or it reported a message not entrusted to writing (Them. *Ep.* 7; the messenger delivered it unaware of its cryptic nature). The recipient solicited the carrier for news quite without the permission or intention of the sender (Seneca *Ep.* 50 1; 47 1; see 1 1).

16. Plu. *Alex.* 39 5. Antiphanes Comicus in his *Sappho* portrays Sappho solving a riddle with these words: "The feminine being (gender), then, is an epistle, the babes within her are the letters [of the alphabet] it carries around; they, though voiceless, talk to

Demosthenes once asked, "What wouldn't a person be capable of doing, who would carry a letter and not deliver it forthwith and conscien-
tiously *(orthōs kai dikaiōs)*?"[17]

But there was another side to the reception of a personal letter. The
message could well be intended for others than the immediate addressee. Greetings were to be shared. In one letter from brother to
brother regarding disposition of property, the writer and his acquaintances send greetings to sixteen individuals and to children three
times, to brothers once, and to wife once.[18] In another letter a student
reports on his studies to his father in one sentence. He adds ten greetings from himself to individuals, and three times others send greetings
to "you all" (the recipients).[19] Furthermore, if the recipient was illiterate, someone had to read the letter aloud; this event likely took place
before assembled family and friends, making the arrival of a letter a social event. Epictetus remarked on the anxiety such a scene could potentially cause:

> [He speaks of] trembling at every message, with my own peace of
> mind depending on letters not my own. Someone has arrived
> from Rome. 'If only there is no bad news!' But how can anything
> bad for you happen in a place, if you are not there? Someone ar-
> rives from Greece. 'If only there is no bad news!' In this way for
> you every place can cause misfortune. Isn't it enough for you to be
> miserable where you are? Must you need be miserable even be-
> yond the seas, and by letter?[20]

Furthermore, when a carrier made a direct delivery an oral report commonly accompanied it. Such reading aloud served several purposes, but

---

whom they desire when far away; yet if another happens to be standing near when it is
read [silently], he will not hear." Athen. *X* 450 E (Gulick).

17. D. *Or.* 34 29. See also E. *IA.* 322-26.

18. *BGU* 601 (= K & W, no. 41).

19. *POxy* 1296 (= K & W, 44). See also *BGU* 423 (K & W 38).

20. Arr. *Epict.* III 24. In *Ep.* 6 Plato commends the addressee and two others in mutual friendship; he writes, "Let this letter be read, if possible, by all three of you gathered
together; if that is not possible, by twos, and as often as you can" (Morrow). Mullins says
that the 1st person singular *(aspazomai)* indicates that the sender expected those greeted
". . . to read the letter (or have it read to them) . . ." (Terence Y. Mullins, "Greeting as a
New Testament Form," *JBL* 87 [1968]: 420).

above all the living voice of the reader underscored the sense of the writer's personal presence, thereby strengthening the relationship between sender and receiver.

2. The Official Letter

The preparation and delivery of official, administrative letters was a well-organized and authorized procedure. The Hellenistic kings and the Roman emperors established highly efficient chanceries under epistolographers of high station, and delivery was secure.[21] There was no official post in the earlier classical period, but written communication between military officers or ambassadors in the field was conducted despite the lack of an established post. One reference tells of a dispatch boat or tender (*hyperetikos,* sc. *keles,* LSD) delivering official letters at sea.[22] Nicias was concerned that in the winter it would take a messenger four months to reach Athens from Sicily.[23] Part of a contention between Demosthenes and Aeschines devolved on a charge that, while on an embassy to Philip, Demosthenes had slipped away from the others and secretly written a report to the Assembly.[24] No mention is made of any official channels for preparing, dispatching, or authenticating such letters. Aristotle describes the proper reception of ambassadors and letters: it was the business of the Prytany, the tribe presiding monthly over the Council and Assembly, to receive heralds and ambassadors for preliminary consultation and to receive letters delivered by them.[25]

The reasons for the failure to establish a postal system in the earlier

---

21. C. Bradford Welles, *Royal Correspondence in the Hellenistic Period: A Study in Greek Epistolography* (New Haven: Yale University Press, 1934; reprint, Chicago: Ares, 1974), xxxvii-xli. (Hereafter Welles, *Royal Cor.*); Fergus Millar, "Emperors at Work," *JRS* 57 (1967): 9-19. For the naming of the envoy see Welles' note on no. 49 line 11 (p. 201); cf. nos. 47, 65, 66, 67.

22. D. *Or.* 50 46. This is the only such record this writer has found, though it must have been a more common practice than indicated. The letter reporting the catastrophe at Arginusae was naturally sent by boat (X. *Hell.* 1 7 4; see the preceding notice to a dispatch boat in 1 6 36; and 1 1 23).

23. Th. 6 21; see the account below.

24. Aeschin. *Or.* 2 128-29.

25. Arist. *Ath.* 43 6.

period must be ascribed to the practice of conducting business of state both internal and external by means of oral speech. There was a general distrust of the written word: Isocrates, obviously referring to literary letters, gives three reasons why it is better to offer advice in person rather than by letter, one of which states that people believe things spoken more readily than things written because they take the spoken word as practical advice but the written as an artistic composition.[26] A postal system was finally established with the rise of Macedon, but details about its operations are scarce. Philip is accredited with the founding of the office of epistolographer in Greece, and a post uniting Alexander's realm is presupposed in a story told by Lucian.[27] Services were also provided on a lesser scale for minor officials and can be described from the papyrus evidence: for example, there were royal secretaries and district and village scribes.[28] There are two receipts from the scribe of the letter-carriers to the royal scribe regarding payment to the carriers.[29] The legible portion of a papyrus fragment of a log from a postal relay station (ca. 255 BCE) lists at least forty-two letters during eight days forwarded through the station.[30]

With regard to reception, administrative communications were directed to a chief officer, a body of people, a state or community, or authorized representatives. Official presentation, public reading, and oral reports constituted a protocol that completed the customary procedures for well-established logistics: preparation, delivery, reception.

The pattern and continuing observance of this protocol is illustrated by two occasions widely differing in time, culture, and setting. One is recorded by Thucydides and the other by Luke. During the Peloponnesian War between Athens and Sparta (Th. 7 8-15), the Athenians sent an ill-fated expedition to Sicily in an attempt to outflank

---

26. Isoc. *Ep.* I 2-3; cf. *Philippus* 25-26; D. *Ep.* I 3.

27. *Rhet. Praec.* 5. See above, note 3.

28. See White, *Light* (above, note 3), nos. 44-51, for royal secretary and district and village scribes.

29. See *BGU* 1232 (K & W, 107).

30. *PHib* 110. See Friedrick Preisigke, "Die ptolemaische Staatspost," *Klio* 7 (1907): 241-77; L. Mitteis und U. Wilchens, *Grundzüge und Chrestomathie der Papyruskunde* (Hildesheim, 1963), I 2, 513-15; also A. H. M. Jones, *OCD*, s.v. "Postal Service (Greek)," and G. H. Stevenson, s.v. "Postal Service (Roman)," 723; O. Seeck, Pauly-W., *RE*, s.v. "Cursus Publicus," IV cols. 2 1846-1863.

the Peloponnesus. The tactic failed. The general Nicias, in desperate straits, sent messengers to Athens to report on conditions. Nicias also sent a letter because he did not trust the messengers to give an accurate report. According to Thucydides,

> The following winter the messengers of Nicias, on reaching Athens, gave the messages which they had been ordered to give by word of mouth, answering any questions that were asked, and delivered the letter. And the clerk of the city came before the Athenians and read them the letter, which runs as follows. . . . (7 10, Smith)

Centuries later this same protocol was observed among the early Christians. After the Jerusalem Conference two men, Judas and Silas, were selected to accompany Barnabas and Paul and to report the decision of the Council to the churches in Antioch and the surrounding region. They carried a letter with them. The letter gives the background for the message, makes mention of Barnabas and Paul, and tells of the election of Judas and Silas, "who themselves will tell you the same things by word of mouth."[31] At the end of the letter in a few words the decree of the Council is appended. The chief purpose of the letter was to authorize the mission of Judas and Silas, Paul and Barnabas. The two pairs of commissioners delivered the report orally and were witnesses to it. Acts continues the account after the men's arrival:

> So they were sent off and went down to Antioch. When they gathered the congregation together, they delivered the letter. When its members read it, they rejoiced at the exhortation. Judas and Silas, who were themselves prophets, said much to encourage and strengthen the believers. (Acts 15:30-32)

In the centuries between Thucydides and Luke, the combination of oral and written word was customary and the protocol of reception was observed similarly. Further evidence of this is supplied by the royal let-

---

31. Acts 15:27. "Judas and Silas (and much more Paul and Barnabas) could no doubt be trusted to emphasize 'by words' to the Gentile Christians what the letter itself very pointedly does not say." Gregory Dix, *Jew and Greek: A Study in the Primitive Church* (Westminster: Dacre Press, 1953), 48.

ters, Josephus, and others. Welles describes the recognition accorded to envoys who carried a letter.[32] The same protocol is recorded for the communication between Darius and Alexander concerning the release of the king's captured family.[33] The author of the fictionalized account of the preparation of the Septuagint is all the more careful to record the observance of the established customs.[34] And from his own experiences in the struggles for control of Galilee Josephus shows that nearly identical procedures were observed.[35]

That official letters to communities were read aloud is well established. The rhetoricians classified the letter with other types of literature to be read aloud, and references in the orators reveal the same practice.[36] A letter from Caracalla permitting a priest to transfer from Sardis to Philadelphia has an appended notation after the date, "Read aloud in the Theater."[37]

Through the centuries, then, in different communities and settings, the official, administrative letter was treated consistently. It was prepared by competent, authorized persons and was carried by envoys who delivered it with ceremony appropriate to the particular assignment. It was addressed and delivered to a constituted body and read before that assembly or its representatives. Carriers also delivered oral messages and answered inquiries related to the letter's content.

---

32. Welles, *Royal Cor.* (above, note 21), p. xxxix and nos. 25, 31, 32, 35, 52 lines 37-41 and 68-72. He says in reference to ll. 68-72, "References in this fashion to an oral message sent through envoys is one of the stock letter endings" (p. 217).

33. Arr. *An.* 2 14 1ff. cf. 10; *Cyr.* 4 5 18-34.

34. J. *Ant.* 11 52, 86.

35. J. *Life* 311-12. See also J. *Ant.* 13 126-29, 145; 1 Macc 11:57; 14:16ff.

36. *Prolegomena Artis Rhetoricae Anonyma* 6 25-27 (Rabe, Tübner, 38-39); see Isoc. *Ep.* I 3; *Philippus* 25-26; Antiphon *Or.* 5 52ff.; D. *Or.* 23 159-64; Demetr. *de Eloc.* 224; J. *Life* 309-31; 2 Baruch 78-86.

37. *SIG* 2 883 (214 CE) = no. 279 (cf. no. 207) in Allan Chester Johnson, Paul Robinson Coleman-Norton, and Frank Card Bourne, *Ancient Roman Statutes* (Austin: University of Texas Press, 1961). See Jeremiah's observance of the protocol, Jer 36:4-8. For the role of envoys in the Greco-Roman world see the definitive study, Margaret M. Mitchell, "New Testament Envoys in the Context of Greco-Roman Diplomatic and Epistolary Conventions: The Example of Timothy and Titus," *JBL* 111 (1992): 641-62. For the Semitic world, Samuel A. Meier, *The Messenger in the Ancient Semitic World,* HSM 45 (Atlanta: Scholars Press, 1988); John T. Greene, *The Role of the Messenger and Message in the Ancient Near East,* BJS 169 (Atlanta: Scholars Press, 1989).

B. Pauline Logistics

1. Preparation

The formulation and recording of Paul's letters was no small task. The penning of a document the length and content of Romans, for example, was a challenge which required planning, drafting, mental and physical labor, and time.[38] Furthermore, Paul did not have a permanent central office equipped with personnel and materials. But even a prison could serve that purpose; Paul nowhere complains about his problems. We know that he was aided by scribes: in addition to the explicit statement by Tertius (Romans 16:22), the phrase "in my own hand" at the conclusion of other letters indicates that an aide was taking dictation at least some of the time.[39]

Paul considered himself to be writing to specific communities. His letters were communal letters addressed to ecclesiae or to house churches to whom he ministered in an authoritative capacity.[40] The addresses vary from letter to letter: some are limited to one congregation (as in 1 Thessalonians); others are widely generalized (Romans or 1 and 2 Corinthians). Some mention specific individuals (Philippians, Philemon); others are meant to be broadly circulated among congrega-

---

38. Stange estimated the time needed to dictate Romans at 11 hrs. 20 mins.; 1 Cor, 10 hrs. 20 mins.; Phil and 1 Thess, 2 hrs. 30 mins. (E. Stange, "Diktierpausen in den Paulusbriefen," *ZNW* 18 [1917]: 107-17). Modified by Roller (Otto Roller, *Das Formular der paulinischen Briefe* [Stuttgart: Kohlhammer, 1933]: 8-14). See Stanislaus Lyennet, "De arte litteras exarandi apud antiques," *VD* 34 (1956): 1-11.

39. See below, note 43.

40. For the possibility that portions of the now composite letters were first directed to groups apart from the full assembly see Wayne A. Meeks, *The First Urban Christians: The Social World of the Apostle Paul* (New Haven: Yale University Press, 1983), 75-77 (hereafter Meeks, *Urban Christians*). The communal address appears consistently regardless of the size or structure of the community. See also Jürgen Becker, *Paul: Apostle to the Gentiles* (Louisville: Westminster/John Knox Press, 1993), 241-55; E. Earl Ellis, "Paul and His Co-Workers," *NTS* 17 (1970-1971): 448-49. Ellis suggests, "The (possibly) composite character of certain letters (e.g. Romans and II Corinthians) may find an explanation along the same lines, i.e. one segment addressed to a special group within the community" (448, note 7). See also Robert J. Banks, *Paul's Idea of Community: The Early House Churches in Their Cultural Setting*, revised and updated edition (Peabody, MA: Hendrickson, 1994); Vincent P. Branick, *The House Church in the Writings of Paul* (Wilmington, DE: Michael Glazier, 1989).

tions (Galatians). But always Paul's letters were meant to be received in and by definable communities.

In like manner, Paul wrote from within a community. He surrounded himself with helpers:[41] co-senders named in the salutation,[42] scribes,[43] greeters from the local congregation, commissioners and visitors from other churches.[44] This group of people provided a kind of voluntary ad hoc secretariat. For example, although Philippians was written from prison, Paul names Timothy as co-sender, acknowledges Epaphroditus, and bears greetings from "the brothers who are with me," and from "all the saints, especially those of Caesar's household" (4:21-22).[45] These indi-

41. Ellis, "Paul and His Co-Workers" (preceding note), 439-40. Venetz collects and analyzes references to co-workers as congregational representatives or congregational emissaries (Hermann-Josef Venetz, "Stephanas, Fortunatus, Achaikus, Epaphroditus, Epaphras, Onesimus & Co. Die Frage nach den Gemeindevertretern und Gemeindegesandten in den paulinischen Gemeinden," in Andreas Kessler, Thomas Ricklin, and Gregor Wurst [eds.], *Peregrina couriositas: Eine Reise durch den orbis antiquus* [Freiburg, Schweiz: Universitätsverlag; Göttingen: Vandenhoeck and Ruprecht, 1994], 13-28).

42. The significance of co-senders is treated in Chapter II, "The Official Letter-Form and the Pauline Letters."

43. Rom 16:22; Paul's own autograph shows that a scribe had aided him; also Gal 6:11; 1 Cor 16:21; Phlm 19; Col 4:18; 2 Thess 3:17. Bahr finds evidence of autographs in letters not now revealing a formal autograph (Gordon J. Bahr, "The Subscriptions in the Pauline Letters," *JBL* 87 [1968]: 27-41). For the autographed closings and a critique of Bahr see pp. 172-81 in Richards, *Secretary* (above, note 1); also Paul J. Achtemeier, "*Omne Verbum Sonat:* The New Testament and the Environment of Late Western Antiquity," *JBL* 109 (1990): 12-13, and the literature cited (add *POxy* 724, 155 CE regarding the apprenticeship of a slave for two years to a teacher of shorthand). Gilliard adds to Achtemeier; see his discussion of silent reading and the literature (Frank D. Gilliard, "More Silent Reading in Antiquity: *Non Omne Verbum Sonabat*," *JBL* 112 [1993]: 689-94). See Chap. II, "The Official Letter-Form and the Pauline Letters," "Subscriptions." Murphy-O'Connor argues that co-senders also served as co-authors for 1 and 2 Cor as well as for 1 and 2 Thess (Jerome Murphy-O'Connor, "Co-Authorship in the Corinthian Correspondence," *RB* 100 [1993]: 562-79). A sentence concluding an earlier article by Bahr still pertains. He wrote, "We know that Paul used a secretary, at least for some of his letters, perhaps for all of them; but we do not know how he used his secretary" (Gordon J. Bahr, "Paul and Letter Writing in the First Century," *CBQ* 28 [1966]: 465-77). Paul's strange silence regarding the role of his co-senders makes this observation still accurate.

44. Chap. III, "The Letters," offers the evidence that "all the brothers with me" of Gal 1:1 formed a delegation from the Galatian churches.

45. In writing 1 Thess Paul and Titus seem to be alone. For Caesar's household see Meeks, *Urban Christians* (above, note 40), 21-22.

viduals combined the dependability and, to some extent, the clerical abilities of epistolographers with the intimacy and concern of literate household servants or friends, thus facilitating the composition of the letters.

2. Delivery

The delivery of Paul's letters was also no easy task. Although Timothy is often named in the headings as a co-sender, it is not possible to identify him as a carrier. In fact, he is usually eliminated from that role. For instance, in writing to Philippi Paul says that he hopes to send Timothy to the congregation soon; but this would not be with the letter, for Timothy was to remain with Paul for an uncertain amount of time (2:19-24). The implication is that the letter would be sent meanwhile.[46] In like manner, according to 1 Thessalonians, Timothy has just returned from Thessalonica, and Paul responds to his good report, but there is no indication that he is to repeat the trip immediately to deliver the letter (3:2, 6). Also, the implication in 1 Corinthians 16:10-11 (cf. 4:17) is that a letter will precede Timothy to Corinth, for Paul admonishes the congregation concerning his later reception.

On the other hand, Titus is known to have served as emissary between the apostle and the Corinthians — at one point Paul is anxiously awaiting a meeting with him on his return from Corinth. Titus' trip and Paul's anxiety were both related to at least one written communication to Corinth. It is implied in 2 Corinthians that Titus had delivered a letter and Paul was waiting for his report concerning its reception (7:5-16; cf. 2:13; 12:17-18). Also, Titus served as leader of the commission for collecting the Relief Fund for the church in Jerusalem. Chapters 8 and 9 of 2 Corinthians encourage the congregation to contribute to the fund, but also serve as a letter of authorization of the commission.[47]

---

46. I interpret 16:10 *(ean de elthēi)* as Timothy's visit "impending," BDF 373; and *epempsa humin* in 4:17 as epistolary aorist (not listed in BDF 334, but note *egrapsa humin*, 5:11). For further discussion concerning dispatch see M. Luther Stirewalt, Jr., "Paul's Evaluation of Letter-Writing," in J. M. Myers, O. Reimherr, and H. N. Bream (eds.), *Search the Scriptures: New Testament Studies in Honor of Raymond T. Stamm* (Leiden: Brill, 1969), 186-88 . See also Martin R. P. McGuire, "Letters and Letter Carriers in Christian Antiquity," *CW* 53 (1960): 148-53, 184-85, 199-200.

47. The relation of 2 Cor 8 and 9 and their possible independence of their present

Such a letter Titus himself would carry. In like manner Epaphroditus ("my fellow worker" and "your messenger," Phil 2:25) would return to Philippi carrying his letter of commendation (2:29). The circulation of a letter like Galatians, addressed to congregations throughout an entire province, required special arrangements for delivery.

The myriad possibilities for delivery of a letter can be illustrated from 1 Corinthians.[48] There were several movements of people between Corinth and Ephesus, where Paul composed the letter; they can be summarized as follows:

Stephanas, Fortunatus, and Achaicus of Corinth are consulting with Paul (16:17-18).[49]

---

context do not affect Titus' role or the authorization of the commission. Dieter Georgi makes a persuasive summary of the evidence for taking the two chapters as remnants of two letters, the one (chap. 8) written to recommend the emissaries, the other (chap. 9) as a circular letter to encourage the contributors. See "A Brief Excursus on the Literary-Critical Problems Inherent in II Corinthians 8 and 9," in *Remembering the Poor: A History of Paul's Collection for Jerusalem* (Nashville: Abingdon, 1992), 75-79. Betz strongly supports the two-letter hypothesis (Hans Dieter Betz, *2 Corinthians 8 and 9: A Commentary on Two Administrative Letters of the Apostle Paul,* Hermeneia [Philadelphia: Fortress, 1985], see esp. 131-40); also, Verlyn Davis Verbrugge, *The Collection and Paul's Leadership of the Church in Corinth* (Ann Arbor: University of Michigan Press, 1988); see his summary of arguments, pp. 87-90. Stowers argues from his interpretation of *peri men gar* that the two chapters form one letter (Stanley K. Stowers, "*Peri men gar* and the Integrity of 2 Cor. 8 and 9," *NovT* 32 [1990]: 340-48). See Nils A. Dahl, "Paul and Possessions," Appendix II, "On the Literary Integrity of 2 Corinthians 1-9," in *Studies in Paul* (Minneapolis: Augsburg, 1977), 38-39. Lodge argues that they are from separate letters (John G. Lodge, "The Apostle's Appeal and the Readers' Response: 2 Corinthians 8 and 9," *Chic. Stud.* 30 [1991]: 59-75). The references to envoys and letters were customary with the Hellenistic kings: Welles, *Royal Cor.* (above, note 21), see p. xxxix and the letters; Acts 15:22-23a. For biographical notes, NT refs., and bibliography regarding Barnabas and Titus see Hans Dieter Betz, *Galatians: A Commentary on Paul's Letter to the Churches in Galatia* (Philadelphia: Fortress, 1979), 84. The *locus classicus* for the combination of embassy and letter is Thucydides 7 10; cf. D. *Or.* 7 *(On Hallonnessus)* sections 19, 46 *et passim.* For studies on messengers and messages see above, note 37.

48. If 1 Cor is composite, these statistics cover a period of time, not one occasion. The listing is revised and condensed from Stirewalt, "Paul's Evaluation of Letter-Writing" (above, note 46), 188-89. See Meeks, *Urban Christians* (above, note 40), "Mobility," 16-17; Gerd Theissen, *The Social Setting of Pauline Christianity: Essays on Corinth* (Philadelphia: Fortress, 1982), "References to Travel," 91-96.

49. For the identification of the delegation from Corinth and Chloe's delegation see

A letter-carrier has made the same trip (7:1).

Timothy is making a round trip between Ephesus and Corinth (16:11).

Apollos will visit Corinth "when he has the opportunity" (16:12).

Brothers have recently gone to Corinth with whom Apollos might have traveled had he not been delayed (16:12).

A letter-carrier is to carry the present writing to Corinth.

There were, then, at least three visitors from Corinth. They could certainly have brought the messages from Corinth (7:1); or they may have carried Paul's letter back to Corinth; they might have done both. Counting only two brothers (there may have been more), there were no less than nine individuals in six parties who were potentially traveling to Corinth. Any of these might have served as carrier.

Thus the problem of the post was solved for Paul by the service of people who supported him and shared his ministry. Some, like Titus, appear to have served him regularly as emissaries; all seem to have been capable and trustworthy — traits that were essential in persons entrusted with the delivery of letters.

3. Reception

The reception of Paul's letters is of particular significance in determining the theory and practice of his epistolary ministry. His letters were addressed and delivered to assemblies of the people. They were publicly read, and oral messages were added; certainly Colossians 4:7-9 describes a Pauline custom.

As noted above, Paul's letters are addressed to whole ecclesiae or to house churches[50] even when he is dealing with one-to-one relationships (Phil 4:2-3; Phlm; cf. Col 4:17) or with factions within a community (1 Cor 3). The communal, inclusive address is expressed in various ways.

Dahl, *Studies in Paul* (above, note 47), "Paul and the Church at Corinth according to 1 Corinthians 1:10–4:21," 50-52. For the identity of Chloe's people: Meeks, *Urban Christians* (above, note 40), 59; Theissen, *Social Setting* (preceding note), 92-94. For the identification of Chloe's delegation *with* the delegation from Corinth, see Chap. III on 1 Corinthians, 72-74.

50. See above, note 40.

Only 1 Thessalonians is limited to a single congregation. The address to the Romans is generalized: "To all God's beloved in Rome." The letter to Galatia circulated through all the congregations of that region. For the reconciliation of Onesimus and Philemon, the latter, two other persons, and the congregation of which Philemon was a member are named. All bishops and deacons are singled out in Philippi, perhaps to aid in easing Epaphroditus' return.[51] Corinth is the key city for the mission to all Achaia; at any time in its assembly one may expect visits from the saints "who in every place call on the name of the Lord" (1:2). In like manner 2 Corinthians extends "to all the saints who are in Achaia" (1:1).[52]

Paul's letters were read aloud.[53] The strongly worded directive in 1 Thessalonians may have set the practice. Paul wrote, "I solemnly command you by the Lord that this letter be read to all of them" (5:27).[54] Other evidence within the letters shows that public reading was antici-

---

51. Bernhard Mayer, "Paulus als Vermittler zwischen Epaphroditus und der Gemeinde von Philippi: Bemerkungen zu Phil. 2, 25-30," *BZ* 31 (1987): 167-88.

52. Oscar Broneer, "Corinth, Center of Paul's Missionary Work in Greece," *BA* 14 (1951); and "The Apostle Paul and the Ismian Games," *BA* 25 (1962); William Baird, *The Corinthian Church — A Biblical Approach to Urban Culture* (New York and Nashville: Abingdon, 1964), 18-28; Meeks, *Urban Christians* (above, note 40), 47-49; Victor Paul Furnish, *II Corinthians*, Anchor Bible (Garden City, NY: Doubleday, 1984), see "Political and Commercial Importance," 7-10.

53. For the practice of reading aloud in the early church, see 1 Tim 4:13; Muratorian Canon in reference to the Shepherd of Hermas, p. 11a = "Appendix C," in B. F. Westcott, *A General Survey of the History of the Canon of the NT,* 6th ed. (New York, 1889), 526-27 and 537-38; Eusebius *HE* V, 12. Cf. *BAG* s.v. *anagnōsis; TDNT* s.v. *legō* 4, 100-101 (Kittel); W. Bauer, *Der Wortgottesdienst der ältesten Christen* (1930), 39-54; O. Cullmann, *Early Christian Worship,* SBT 10 (London: SCM Press, 1953), 20-25. Collins suggests that Paul may have wanted to introduce a service based on that of the synagogue and that public reading was an early step toward the development of Christian Scripture (Raymond F. Collins, "'... that this letter be read to all the brethren.' A New Testament Note," *LS* 9 [1982]: 123; reprint 365-70 in Raymond F. Collins [ed.], *Studies on the First Letter to the Thessalonians,* BETL 66 [Leuven: Leuven University Press, 1984]). Hartman thinks that Paul's letters, contrary to personal letters, were read in ever wider circles (L. Hartman, "On Reading Others' Letters," *HTR* 79 [1986]: 137-46). See also H. J. B. Combrink, "The Role of the Reader and Other Literary Categories in Philippians," *Scriptura* 20 (1987): 33-40; Fred B. Craddock, *Philippians* (Atlanta: John Knox, 1985), 4-9. For the reception of secular letters see below, note 69; for OT see 2 Kgs 19:8-14 = Is 37:8-14; cf. Ezra 4:17-24.

54. The public reading and exchange of letters between Thessalonica and Laodicea, if not an authentic remnant, may be an admonition by Paul's successors to continue the practice for their communications (Col 4:7-9).

pated. The inclusive, corporate nature of the salutations is repeated throughout and implies and requires the public reading of the letters. Paul's favorite term of direct address is *adelphoi*,[55] and he calls upon whole congregations by name, "Corinthians," "Galatians," "Philippians."[56] The congregation is visualized as gathered and set apart from people outside.[57] Parentheses,[58] rhetorical questions,[59] and figures of speech[60] embrace the whole group. Thanksgivings, prayers, and benedictions are phrased on behalf of the local congregation, and requests for prayers by the group are made in turn.[61] Imperatives are phrased to encourage internal, mutual admonition;[62] praise, condemnation, and moral directives are to be endorsed and enforced by congregational sanction.[63] Individual messages in a letter require the attention of an assembly.[64] In addition, the recipients of a letter are to exchange greetings and sometimes the holy kiss.[65] The mutual exchange of word and kiss could be done only in an assembly of people by whom the liturgical rubric was observed.[66] Paul's insistence on the public reading of his

55. He uses it more than 60 times. See especially Rom 7:1; 11:25; 12:1; 16:17; 1 Cor 1:10; 3:1; 4:6; 7:29; 10:1; 11:33; 14:39; 15:1; 15:58; 2 Cor 1:8; 13:11; Gal 1:11; 4:31; 6:1; Phil 1:12; 3:1; 4:1; 4:8; 1 Thess 2:1; 4:1; 5:4; 2 Thess 2:1; 2:13.

56. Gal 3:1; 2 Cor 6:11; Phil 4:15; see also "beloved" 1 Cor 10:14; 2 Cor 7:1; Phil 4:1; et al.

57. 1 Thess 4:9-12; Col 4:5. Meeks, *Urban Christians* (above, note 40), "The Language of Separation," 94-96.

58. E.g., 1 Cor 1:14-16; 1 Thess 4:1. See Section D, below.

59. Esp. Gal 3:2-5; 1 Cor 6:1-6; 2 Cor 11:7-11; Rom 3; 7:7-25.

60. E.g., 1 Cor 12:27 (body of Christ).

61. 1 Thess 5:25; Rom 15:30-33; Phlm 22b; Col 4:2-4.

62. 1 Thess 4:18; 5:11; 1 Cor 1:26; Rom 12; 15:7.

63. E.g., the treatment of the immoral man at Corinth (1 Cor 5:1-2). Note also that Paul's biographical reminiscences are for public presentation, ". . . for I would have you know . . ." Gal 1:11; cf. 2 Cor 11:16ff.; Phil 3:4-6.

64. Phil 4:2-3 (Euodia and Syntyche); Col 4:17 (Archippus). For the possibility that such individual messages were originally directed to a limited group see above, note 40.

65. Greetings were sent from individuals to congregations (Rom 16:5); between two congregations (Rom 16:16; 1 Cor 16:19; 2 Cor 13:12); between individual members of two congregations (Phlm 23-24); from scribe to recipients (Rom 16:22; cf. *Mar. Polycarp* 20:2); from Paul to individuals (Rom 16 *et passim*); from Paul to groups (Rom 16:11); the holy kiss: Rom 16:16; 1 Thess 5:26; see Karl-Martin Hofmann, *Philema hagion* (Gütersloh, 1938), 6, 23-26.

66. But see Terence Y. Mullins, "Greeting as a New Testament Form," *JBL* 87 (1968): 426. Collins writes, "At the outset, however, it would appear that the invitation to greet one another with a holy kiss was more in the nature of a request that greeting be extended than it was a liturgical directive" (R. F. Collins, *Studies* [above, note 53], 138-39).

letters whether in a full assembly or in household meetings merits special notice. A letter was not circulated among individuals nor only
posted for their reading; it was directed to an assembly. Reading aloud
re-animated the written word and secured the sense of the writer's
presence.[67]

Trusted emissaries customarily also carried oral messages. Paul sent
Timothy only with oral word to Thessalonica, "to strengthen and encourage you for the sake of your faith" (1 Thess 3:2); and to Corinth, "to
remind you of my ways in Christ Jesus as I teach them everywhere in every church" (1 Cor 4:17). Also in his struggle with the Corinthians, dual
commissioners, Titus and the brother, were sent to effect reconciliation
(2 Cor 12:17-18).[68] The members of the Famine Relief Commission delivered both oral and written word (2 Cor 8–9). By the letter Paul recommends the commission of which Titus was leader (8:6, 16-17, 23), explains and endorses their mission, and adds his name to the cause. He
also relies on their oral appeal. He makes it appear that he considers his
written statement secondary to their oral word, for he writes, "Now it is
not necessary for me to write to you about the ministry to the
saints . . ." (9:1); and, "So I thought it necessary to urge the brothers to
go on ahead to you, and arrange in advance for this bountiful gift . . ."
(9:5). These commission members carried the letter, but they were emissaries, not postmen. The oral ministry of such co-workers was an integral component of Paul's total ministry.

One question remains concerning secular, official letters and Paul's
letters. Who read the letters aloud? We know, for example, that the
Athenian Assembly employed a clerk to present letters aloud. Elsewhere
Xenophon makes reference to a letter-carrier being used as a reader.[69]

---

67. See above, note 53.

68. The explicit statement regarding an oral report in Col 4:7 ("Tychicus will tell you
all the news about me") may have been written to encourage the church to continue nar-
rating oral history.

69. X. *Hell.* 7 1 39; cf. Th. 8 8-15; D. *Or.* 18 39 *et passim.* Aristotle, regarding the reception of ambassadors and letters, makes no reference to readers (*Ath.* 43 6, above, note 25).
One must assume a well known practice, perhaps a designated reader. For the public
reading of Demosthenes' letters see Jonathan A. Goldstein, *The Letters of Demosthenes*
(New York: Columbia University Press, 1968), 129-30. See also G. L. Hendrickson, "Ancient Reading," *Class. Journ.* 25 (1929/30): 182-84; W. P. Clark, "Ancient Reading," *ibid.* 26
(1930/31): 698-700; McGuire (above, note 46) refers to J. Balogh, "Voces paginarum,
Beitrage zur Geschichte des Lauten Lesens und Schreibens," *Philol* 82 (1927): 202-40. See

In these cases someone of position and capable of the task was recognized as public reader. Achtemeier has pointed out that, since words were written with no spaces between them in Paul's day, it was imperative that a public reader be given opportunity to acquaint himself with a letter's content beforehand.[70]

For Paul's letters no reader is designated. The adjuration at the close of 1 Thessalonians is given in the passive voice: "I solemnly command you [pl.] by the Lord that this letter be read [*anagnōsthēnai*] to all the members" (5:27). The charge is given to the whole congregation, and no reader is named. Given its early date of composition, it is unlikely that the recipients of 1 Thessalonians would have known immediately how Paul wished it to be presented. Thus the carrier may have been instructed to read the letter himself or to see to it that a capable person — perhaps the one presiding at the assembly or a designated reader — make the presentation. In either case, applying Achtemeier's observation, the one expecting to read the letter must have spent some time with the writing before the congregation was assembled.

Some evidence may be derived from the apostrophes addressed to individuals within the letters and from Philemon. Philemon is addressed to a congregation; its salutation is in the customary plural. The body of the letter (4-21) is in the singular, referring to Philemon. At the close, Paul expresses confidence in Philemon and requests of him the preparation of a guest room. Immediately thereafter the request for prayers is made in the plural, that is, to the whole congregation once again. The greetings that follow are directed only to Philemon; the benediction reverts to the plural. It is clear that in this letter the singular address to Philemon takes place in a corporate liturgical setting. Furthermore, the letter is a letter of commendation for Onesimus. He, therefore, carries the letter. He delivers it to Philemon, who of necessity will acquaint himself with the content and read it in the congregational setting within which Paul visualized its reception.[71]

Paul J. Achtemeier, *"Omne Verbum Sonat . . . ,"* and Frank D. Gilliard, *". . . Non Omne Verbum Sonabat"* (above, note 43).

70. Achtemeier observes that it was important for someone acquainted with the content to read the letter in public. Such preparation would overcome the difficulty to reader and listeners caused by the continuous flow of lines and alphabetic letters (Paul J. Achtemeier, *"Omne Verbum Sonat . . ."* [above, note 43], 17-19).

71. See Chap. III, "The Letters," 93-94.

A similar setting occurs in Philippians. Between the closing admonitions, ". . . stand firm . . ." and ". . . rejoice . . ." (4:1 and 4), Paul makes his request to an individual with whom he is well acquainted,

> I urge Euodia and Syntyche to be of the same mind in the Lord. Yes, and I ask you also, my loyal companion, to help these women. . . . (4:2-3)

Reconciliation between the two women is to be undertaken immediately in the congregational setting, and the companion (Syzygos) who is presiding and reading the letter must initiate the effort.[72]

Thus it seems clear that Paul made the congregation responsible for the public reading of his letters. The actual reading was done by prominent members such as Philemon and the companion mentioned in Philippians. It was not a matter of indifference to Paul nor was it left to chance. He was assured of the public reading of his letters.

C. Conclusion

It is at once obvious that the fortuitous logistics upon which the commoner had to rely for the preparation and delivery of personal letters were wholly inadequate for the conduct of Paul's epistolary ministry. The communications were directed to assemblies, ecclesiae, whose functioning, continuing existence, and faithful adherence to the gospel, required directives and decisions; and in relation to them Paul felt an authoritative calling. For conducting such a ministry the logistics of personal letter writing offered no really reliable or consistently available model.

On the other hand official, administrative correspondence offered Paul a basic model of logistics which he could adapt for his purposes. He was well acquainted with official correspondence.[73] According to

---

72. According to Colossians this kind of congregational support was continued. If it is not an old Pauline admonition still unfulfilled, someone else wrote, "And say to Archippus, 'See that you [sing.] complete the task that you have received in the Lord'" (4:17).

73. See 1 Cor 7:1; 16:3; Acts 18:27; 23:25-30; 28:21; See Chap. II, "The Official Letter-Form and the Pauline Letters." Paul was trained in rabbinic polity and administration. Wuellner, referring to Daube and Lieberman (*Niddah* 70b), notes that halakic discus-

the book of Acts, he held an official position in the Jewish community in which official letter-writing was an administrative instrument: He was authorized by a letter from the high priest to seize Christians at Antioch (9:1-2). He was a member of the embassy which carried to Antioch the letter reporting the decision of the Jerusalem Conference (15:22-35). Chapters 8–9 of 2 Corinthians authorize a commission to collect contributions to the Relief Fund. The metaphor he presents to the Corinthian congregation is that of a letter written not on stone but on the human heart (3:1-3); the metaphor refers to inscribed letters that were of official origin. He likely saw many of them along the roadways and in the cities of his travels.

Paul's logistics were modeled on the official letter setting. A staff of volunteers supported him; some of them contributed to the formulation of messages, while others aided in the actual writing. His post was an organized and dependable service. He did not depend on hired carriers or slaves, nor upon the chance journeying of friends or strangers. He relied on people who shared his work and therefore had an investment in the communications necessitated by his circuit-riding ministry. As shown by his arrangements for delivery, when a letter left Paul's hand, he was assured of its delivery. The planning and purpose of logistics are completed by the letter's reception; preparation and dispatch are directed to this end. Paul's letters were received by the officers and people of an ecclesia, an organized body. Oral reading and additional oral messages publicized and confirmed the message but also transmitted the sender's apostolic authority and made the recipients responsible for observing the directives contained in the letter.

Paul's solution to the logistic problems gave him control of the total letter setting. His supervising of preparation and delivery and the certainty of reception provided security for the development of his epistolary ministry.

---

sions were conducted by letter (Wilhelm Wuellner, "Haggadic Homily Genre in I Corinthians 1-2," *JBL* 89 [1970]: 203). Pastoral letters were issued by the rabbis (Hugo Mantel, *Studies in the History of the Sanhedrin* [Cambridge, MA: Harvard University Press, 1961], 190-95; Jacob Neusner, *A Life of Rabban Johanan ben Zakkai ca. 1-80 C.E.* ([Leiden: Brill, 1962; 2nd ed. rev. 1973], 22-23). For references to the problem of delivery see *Tem.* 14a (Epstein, *The Babylonian Talmud* 98); *Sab.* 10, 4; *Sab.* 19a (Epstein, 78-79) gives the regulations for dispatching mail by Gentile hands at the approach of the Sabbath. See *TDNT* 7, 594 (Rengsdorf).

D. Some Evidences of Paul's Preparation of the Letters

Letter writing is the confining of thought and word in a practical and material medium for the communication of messages between separated parties. For Paul's purposes, thought and word like new wine had to be bottled in the new wineskin of the apostolic letter in order to be sent to the churches. A revealing factor in the writing of any letter is the writer's immersion in, and accommodation of, the demands of the letters' logistics. The writer's response to such challenges reveals characteristics of his or her method.

Some expressions in the Pauline letters reveal a practice of extemporary composition. For example, in a conversational manner Paul makes spontaneous corrections or amendments to his statements while writing or dictating. Note the correction of personal pronouns in passing,

> . . . we wanted to come to you — certainly I, Paul, wanted to again and again. . . . (1 Thess 2:18)

> . . . we decided to be left alone in Athens; and we sent Timothy. . . . For this reason, when I could bear it no longer, I sent to find out about your faith. (3:1-2, 5)

> To the married I give this command — not I but the Lord. . . . To the rest I say — I and not the Lord. . . . (1 Cor 7:10, 12)

Parentheses disclose Paul's extemporary composition. He hesitates and corrects his recollection of baptisms at Corinth (1 Cor 1:14-16). He does not want the Thessalonians to infer that, as he had formerly taught them, they are not now living as they ought and pleasing God; so he must add parenthetically, "as in fact, you are doing" (1 Thess 4:1). In one paragraph in Galatians, while recalling his early experiences, he interjects three explanatory parentheses, for example, ". . . I laid before them (though only in a private meeting with the acknowledged leaders) the gospel . . ." (2:2).[74]

---

74. Without regard for Paul's extempore composition BDF says regarding parentheses, "The NT, especially the Epistles of Paul, contain a variety of parentheses, harsher than a careful stylist would allow. Since Paul's train of thought in general includes many and long digressions . . . it is not surprising that his sentence structure even in narrower

Similarly, anacolutha — inconsistent grammatical constructions — reveal Paul's extempore method of composition. BDF uses Galatians 2:6 as an example of an anacoluthon after an intervening clause or sentence; literally in English,

> From those supposed to be something
> — whatever they were makes no difference to me.
>   God shows no partiality. —
> Those supposed ones contributed nothing to me.[75]

And again, in 2 Corinthians 5:12,

> We do not commend ourselves to you again,
> but giving you an opportunity to boast about us. . . .

A revision might change the participle to a finite verb,

> We do not commend ourselves, but we give you opportunity. . . .

Or as BDF suggests (scil 'we write this'),

> We do not commend ourselves . . ., but we write this giving you an opportunity. . . .

In addition to these grammatical oddities, the letters contain a kind of anacoluthon of ideas that suggests that they underwent little revision. Writers who know their readers well often simply record their thoughts as they come to mind, knowing the readers will be able to contextualize them. This seems to have been the case with Paul — and since the letters to him from the churches are lost to us today, how can

---

contexts is not uninterrupted: e.g. Rom 1:13 . . ." (465, pp. 242-43). See Gal 1:20; 1 Cor 11:33-34 and other references in *BDF* 465. Some parentheses are not so disruptive in the context being more integral to the line of thought; e.g. Rom 5:7; 7:1; 10:6-8; 2 Cor 11:17; Phlm 11. However, Paul must make clear at once his relation to the law, 1 Cor 9:20b-21.

75. Again BDF does not allow for the extempore composition of the letters. They say concerning this type of anacoluthon and using Gal 2:6 for the example, "The narrative parts of the NT do not contain many anacolutha of this type. They are more numerous and flagrant in the Pauline Epistles, although the Epistles are uneven in this respect since the care with which they were composed varies considerably: G 2:6 . . ." (467, p. 245). See also from BDF 457, 2 Cor 7:5; 8:18ff.; 9:11; Rom 12:9ff.; Phil 1:29-30.

we wonder overmuch at the occasional difficulty of following Paul's chain of thought? In addition, pauses and interruptions must have occurred during preparation, fragmenting somewhat any predetermined sequence. Consider, for example, Paul's deeply affectionate engagement with the Philippians:[76] he describes his present situation; records the Christ hymn; commends Timothy and Epaphroditus; warns about evil workers; admonishes Euodia and Syntyche; reviews his relationship with the Philippians; expresses thanks for the gift; even admits a rough transition (3:1ff.). This is not to say that Paul did not organize his thoughts to some extent before writing them down (or enlisting someone to take dictation). But it suggests that they were written down knowing that their readers would be able to quickly make connections that are difficult for us today.

Another example of extempore production may be seen in the chains of metaphors that appear to come spontaneously from Paul's mind; for example, triumphal procession, aroma of incense, peddlers, letter of recommendation (2 Cor 2:14–3:3). He finally selects and expands on the letter of recommendation (see chapter IV, section C for more on this). In like manner the Corinthians are a plant, a field, a building (1 Cor 3:5-9). Paul expands the building metaphor (vv. 10-15), and the building is then designated a temple (vv. 16-17).

These characteristics become more discernible when viewed within the larger context of Pauline letter writing. The letters are part of an interrupted but ongoing conversation with the churches; they are responses to oral and written reports from the people — the oral by his own emissaries or by representatives from the churches. As continued conversation the letters were prepared with an immediacy peculiar to their situation, even with a tentativeness in expectation of continuing dialogue in person or by letter or emissary.[77] It is in this context that

---

76. For a rhetorical analysis see Duane F. Watson, "A Rhetorical Analysis of Philippians and Its Implication for the Unity Question," *NovT* 30 (1988): 57-88. Watson gives an accounting for each section of the letter by specific rhetorical topics, devices, etc., derived from the rhetoricians. On this analysis he bases his decision regarding the unity of the letter. He classifies Phil as deliberative rhetoric in answer to one question, "What is the manner of life worthy of the gospel? (1:27-30)," p. 60. See his explanation on rhetorical basis for the section 3:1ff., pp. 84-87. Watson makes no mention of the epistolary context of Phil.

77. Paul recalls or anticipates continued conversation by himself in person: 1 Cor

Paul corrects himself in the midst of writing or dictating without later revision, and he can forward corrections to the people's misunderstanding whether about a moral problem or his own change of plans.

The temporal factor of delayed conversation and the physical factor of separation combine to require arrangements for delivery and presentation. As demonstrated above, Paul adapted the official letter's logistics for his communications. In other words, his missives were carried by a responsible party who became the surrogate — the personal representative — of the sender. In Paul's case the functions of carrier and/or reader are not explicitly described, but one or both, carrier or presenter, would have become his personal representative before the people. In the secular realm the carrier was an envoy who was informed and responsible for interpretation, expected to speak for and report back to the sender. Enough evidence has been gleaned from Paul's letters to conclude that he arranged similar assignments to complete the letter-event. The service of a personal surrogate was of special significance for Paul. Stanley K. Stowers summarizes the role when noting the presence or absence of writer or speaker as one way in which writing differs from speech. He says, ". . . there are important communicative aspects of personal presence that are not part of writing, for example, inflection, tone, gesture, overt emotional behavior."[78]

Such personal aspects the reader supplied, and Paul was certainly conscious of the shift in personnel required for the oral delivery of his message. He must have known that presenters would inevitably color the message with their own personal aspects and speech habits. Separated from the people, confronted by the necessary temporal delays, Paul depended on a third party to complete and update communications and to return messages from the correspondents — to expand and interpret his written word, and to translate his thought and intention when the messages were presented orally before an assembly.

11:34; 2 Cor 9:5; 10:11; 12:14; Phil 1:27; by emissary: Phil 2:19; 2 Cor 8:16, 22; 12:18; by letter: 1 Cor 5:9; ref. to letter from Corinth: 1 Cor 7:1.

78. Stanley K. Stowers, "Social Typification and the Classification of Ancient Letters," in Jacob Neusner et al. (eds.), *The Social World of Formative Christianity and Judaism in Tribute to Howard Clark Kee* (Philadelphia: Fortress, 1988), 78-90; quotation from p. 79. See also Hans Dieter Betz, *Galatians: A Commentary on Paul's Letter to the Churches in Galatia*, Hermeneia (Philadelphia: Fortress, 1979), 24. Betz does not take into consideration the oral reading of a letter before a congregation.

The logistics for the preparation, dispatch, and reception of letters define the context and identify the genre of the document. They also influence the writer's method of composition. Immediate corrections, parentheses, and anacolutha give evidence that the initial drafts of Paul's epistles were not revised. They reflect a sense of urgency — either from the presence of emissaries waiting to return home to deliver the letter and make their reports (1 Corinthians, Galatians, Philippians), or in light of the knowledge that communication by letter always involved a hiatus of contact. The evidence also shows that the writer, having once accepted the medium, could not suppress an enthusiasm for writing and a pleasure in the opportunity to fulfill his office.

Beyond logistics, Paul adapted the official epistolary form and function in order to create an apostolic letter for preserving and administering the congregations, for their instructions and liturgical development, and for maintaining personal relationships and corporate consciousness.

II

The Official Letter-Form
and the Pauline Letters

A. Introduction

As a highly literate person corresponding with geographically scattered groups of people, Paul was deeply enmeshed in the communicative world of his day. He was, therefore, exposed to the forms, functions, and settings of the various types of letters that were being written. It is the purpose of this chapter to show that Paul absorbed from this environment some units and uses out of the broad field of official correspondence just as he did from personal correspondence. The forms and functions of both types were freely available to him, and he drew upon them, consciously or otherwise, when he realized the necessity of resorting to letter writing and as he developed the apostolic letter in the conduct of his ministry.

This initial study faces two major obstacles. First, the extensive field of official letter writing has been largely neglected by both ancient and modern commentators. Also, Paul's uses of epistolary conventions are regularly modified by the demands of his unique ministry, by his theological commitments, and by his personal creativity. And yet two a priori considerations encourage the inquiry. Paul saw himself as a representative of Christ ministering between the Lord and the people of the ecclesiae. It was an authoritative position in the religious community similar to that of numerous officials in the secular world.[1] In addition, he knew and used the official letter on various occasions in his life.[2]

It must be said that neither in form, nor function, nor style can Paul's letters be contained in one category. A person of authority writing communal letters on subjects dealing with faithful adherence to the gospel, polity, ethics, and so on is not writing in a category limited to the maintenance of friendship, the sending of information or a request, and the exchange of greetings. Nor does a person of dedicated ministry and deep personal relationships write only from a detached position on subjects limited to the administration of a jurisdictional unit. Paul's letters fit exclusively in neither normative classification, yet both left their influence on him.

Furthermore, isolating the formal sources of Paul's letters detracts from their integrity. Paul visualized the ministerial needs confronting him and adopted, molded, and devised a communicative form equal to the challenge. It was a medium combining those forms of written communication with which he was acquainted and which he modified and embellished from other resources and, as already noted, by his own creativity and theological convictions. The Pauline letters arose in a unique epistolary setting and may be said to constitute an addition to the epistolary corpus.[3]

1. See, John L. White, *The Apostle of God: Paul and the Promise of Abraham* (Peabody, MA: Hendrickson, 1999), 130-35.

2. For Paul's acquaintance with official letters see Chap. I, "Logistics," 18-19.

3. The official influence is prominent in Paul's salutations, and his freedom of composition vis-à-vis both official and personal conventions is seen in his disregard of the number and choice of topics and the letter's length as required by Demetrius for personal letters and as customary in official letters. Paul's creative adaptation of units and selections from the normative types may be represented by the thanksgiving, the salutation, and the greeting. Concerning the thanksgiving, Paul Schubert concluded, "This observation calls emphatic and convincing attention to the fact that Paul's letters — both functionally and formally — occupy a position between the epigraphical documents (which were intended for publication) and the humble though formal and intimate private letters (which were intended merely for the addressee). . . ." Paul Schubert, *Form and Function of the Pauline Thanksgivings* (Berlin: Töpelmann, 1939), 182. Both Schubert and O'Brien see the thanksgivings as previewing the themes of the letters. See Peter Thomas O'Brien, *Introductory Thanksgivings in the Letters of Paul* (Leiden: Brill, 1977). "The transformation of the terse salutation, 'A to B *chairein*,' to any of Paul's salutations discloses more creativity than an analysis of the formal antecedents can explain." Judith M. Lieu, "'Grace to You and Peace': The Apostolic Greeting," *BJRL* 86

B. The Classification of Greek Official Letters

There are any number of ways to limit what constitutes an "official" letter.[4] But for this chapter a broad and inclusive category is conceived. The business of state is conducted by many people: by the highest officials, subordinate officials responsible only to a higher authority, intermediate officials responsible to a higher authority and to a jurisdictional unit; by numerous magistrates, military officers, and ambassadors. Some official characteristics can be identified in letters written by prominent citizens to political bodies and in those written by ordinary citizens requesting official action or fulfilling legal requirements. Even private citizens either by necessity or courtesy adopt elements of the official form established by professional epistolographers. As will be demonstrated below, through the years and in differing societies the need and purpose of particular units and formulae remain constant — for example, a petitioning Greek citizen and a Roman strategus would identify themselves similarly and for similar reasons. Even the writers of fictitious letters, now included in the histo-

---

(1985): 161-78. Quotation from p. 178. See also E. Lohmeyer, "Probleme paulinischer Theologie I: Die brieflicher Grüssüberschriften," *ZNW* 26 (1927): 158-73. Greeting is a common unit in personal letters and is sometimes sent in official letters. For example, from the Hellenistic letters, "We have ordered Hegestratus to address you at great length on the subject and to give you our greeting. Farewell." Welles, no. 14. Welles remarks, "Diplomatic 'greeting' is often mentioned in the Hellenistic period. Cf. 52, 30 and *SIG* 671 B, 8/9 (Delphi, about 160 B.C.) . . ." (Welles, *Royal Cor.*, p. 77). This is diplomatic courtesy, not the expression of personal friendship in the familiar letters. For greeting in personal letters see Terence Y. Mullins, "Greeting as a New Testament Form," *JBL* 87 (1968): 418-26. Mullins studies exclusively the personal letter. Artimedorus Daldianus emphasized the personal nature of the greeting and farewell and the sharing of them by reading aloud (*Onirocriton* 3 44). Paul's greetings, with some exceptions, and his expressions of affection are addressed to the members of an ecclesia as a body, neither personally intimate nor officially distant.

4. Kim and White write, "The word 'official' is equivalent to 'administrative,' i.e., any correspondence which concerns the bureaucratic system in Egypt, be it at the level of the diocetes or the lowliest village functionary, is considered official. The word official is sometimes applied to letters to or from Hellenistic kings, but it seems preferable to use the designation 'royal,' at least for the diplomatic correspondence, for these letters" (Chan-Hie Kim and John L. White, *Letters from the Papyri: A Study Collection*, Consultation on Ancient Epistolography, SBL Epistolography Seminar, 1974 [unpublished], 8-9; hereafter = K & W.) For the broad survey of this chapter I use an inclusive definition.

ries and orations, observe some of the official conventions, most of which were developed by royal epistolographers.

According to Robert Sherk, these Roman scribes most likely used Greek correspondence as their model:

> In external form, therefore, these Roman letters followed Hellenic models. The agreements are too striking to explain in any other way. In the face of the evidence it would not be rash to maintain that the Romans learned the art of letter writing from the Greeks. Whatever the earlier forms and models might have been before the third century B.C., they soon yielded to the well-finished and highly polished products from the Hellenistic chanceries.[5]

It is the contention of this chapter that the influence of the royal epistolographers became universal during the centuries surrounding Paul's life. However inexactly applied and necessarily modified, they set the model for official Greek-language communication. They established epistolary conventions and etiquette in their field in the same manner in which standards were established for personal letter writing. The letters of political officials were widely available as models: they were heard in public readings and displayed in temples, in other buildings, and along the highways. One collection of letters was inscribed and displayed a century and a half after the event which it commemorated, a fact that witnesses to the continuing pertinence of such letters and their commanding presence.[6] Formal conventions, once established and widely disseminated, profoundly affected official correspondence for both the governing and the governed.

Within this broad activity Paul is a private citizen in the secular po-

---

5. Robert K. Sherk, *Roman Documents from the Greek East: Senatus Consulta and Epistulae to the Age of Augustus* (Baltimore: Johns Hopkins Press, 1969), 197; cf. p. 209. Hereafter Sherk, *Roman Documents*.

6. Welles writes concerning nos. 55-61, "The most striking case is that of the collection 55-61, inscribed on the walls of the temple at Pessinus at least a century and a half after the letters were written. There is no reason to suppose that they had ever been published before" (Welles, *Royal Cor.,* xli). For the dominant influence of the royal letters see Betz' discussion. He adds to the accidence of their widespread survival their "common setting in legal and administrative practices of the day." Hans Dieter Betz, *2 Corinthians 8 and 9: A Commentary on Two Administrative Letters of the Apostle Paul* (Philadelphia: Fortress, 1985), 134. Hereafter, Betz, *2 Corinthians 8–9.*

litical order, but he is an official in the religious citizenry. Within the divine organization he is an intermediary official representing a higher authority — Christ — and at the same time ministering to a jurisdiction — that under Christ's reign. He inevitably incorporates features of official letter writing.[7]

Paul was also acquainted, from his early life, with the uses of the letter in Jewish society, and it is worth noting that he may have been influenced to a certain extent by its conventions. For example, sender identity and co-senders are conventions in Jewish letter writing just as they are in Greco-Roman epistolography. But the two societies conceived of church, state, and the relationship between the two in very different ways, and this is reflected in their official correspondence. Irene Taatz defines the Jewish order in terms of a more naturalistic concept.[8] She finds two classes of official letters differing in their basis of authority. There are those based on the executive authority of officials in Jerusalem; they deal with temple tax, calendar adjustments, and other administrative matters. Then there are those of a more prophetic nature based more immediately on divine authority, which convey religious instruction. Both served to maintain ties between Jerusalem and Diaspora communities. This conception of political order, however, is limited to the Jewish communities and is incompatible with Paul's vision of the Christian community to which he was called to minister. His

7. Concerning Paul's position in authorizing the Relief Commission Betz says, "2 Cor 8 . . . is an official letter sent by an individual writing in an official capacity to a corporate body, the church at Corinth, along with officially appointed envoys. . . . Here church officials function in much the same way as the heads of the various community organizations, clubs, and religious groups. . . . Naturally, this social officialdom must be distinguished from the governmental system which presided over the state, provinces, and cities" (Betz, *2 Corinthians 8–9* [preceding note], 134). See his discussion of official letter writing in connection with his analysis of 1 Cor 8–9, 134-40. The purpose of this chapter is to show Paul's involvement in the "social officialdom" throughout his letter writing.

8. Irene Taatz, *Frühjüdische Briefe: Die paulinische Briefe im Rahmen der offiziellen religiösen Briefe des Frühjudentums*, NTOA 16 (Freiburg, Schweiz: Universitätsverlag; Göttingen: Vandenhoeck and Ruprecht, 1991), 104. Taatz finds that both influenced Pauline form and function. Her study is the counterpart of this one: I present the influence of the Greek official letter; she presents the influence of the Jewish letter. The cosmopolitan culture of the day provided the opportunity for cross cultural influences and thus for Paul's creative letter writing. For the Roman influence on Paul's idea of the basileia see John L. White, *The Apostle of God: Paul and the Promise of Abraham* (above, note 1).

work seems deeply influenced by the breadth and inclusiveness of the Roman order; it is safe to conclude that the Jewish official letter played a very secondary role in his development of the apostolic letter.

Using the inclusive category of official letters and recognizing the interplay and influence of cross-cultural sources, three general classes of official letters may be described: (1) those that clearly substitute for a speech which in other circumstances would have been delivered in person before a constituted body (for example, the Athenian Assembly); (2) those that deal with executive or administrative matters and are addressed only to officials or to officials and communities; (3) those from citizens to officials. Subdivisions are listed in the outline below.

The letters of the first class predominated in the age of the city-states. They were used on occasions when a speaker was unable to deliver his speech orally and in person. The business of a city-state was conducted in the assembly chiefly by deliberative oratory. When it became necessary for separated parties to communicate in writing, the composition was a delayed speech, which, nevertheless, could not escape the epistolary context. Demosthenes set a precedent for these letters: formally they are epistolographical and rhetorical products, and may be called spoken letters.[9]

The letters of the second class functioned in quite a different setting from that of the spoken letters. The demise of the democratic city-states and the rise of Philip and the Hellenistic kings required the development of a new kind of letter — one suited to conducting the affairs of state in a larger kingdom. This class is represented by letters of the Hellenistic kings and Roman officials in the east. They were executive or administrative in intent. This class also includes letters, chiefly from the papyri, dealing with the daily conduct of business among lesser officials.

The basic style of the first class is oratorical or rhetorical. Spoken letters reveal the convergence of speech making and letter writing in an age when the spoken word still held precedent over the written word. Epistolary logistics were imposed on the speech, but only as a result of the need to deliver the message in written form between separated parties.[10] The

9. Schnider and Stenger use the term *Redeersatz* (Franz Schnider and Werner Stenger, *Studien zum neutestamentlichen Briefformular*, NTTS 11 [Leiden: Brill, 1987], 26).

10. See Julian Victor, *Ars Rhetorica*, 27, in Abraham J. Malherbe, *Ancient Epistolary Theorists*, SBLSBS 19 (Atlanta: Scholars Press, 1988), 62-63. In regard to this type it was noted

purpose of the second class is executive or administrative, and the style dialogical (though in the case of executive orders it occasionally becomes monological). These letters initiate or maintain conversations, and their style of dialogue was eminently suited to Paul's communication with the churches.[11]

The third class of letters, from private citizens to officials, was naturally influenced by official conventions. This class encompasses a wide variety of letters, from Demosthenes' letters to the Athenian Assembly, which represent the earlier, rhetorically influenced style, to simple papyrus petitions written with non-rhetorical directness.

The following outline spells out as clearly as possible the three classifications and their subsets — recognizing, of course, that the types of official letters are myriad and yield only to the most general attempts at classification. It includes relevant examples from inscriptions, papyri, and literary sources; asterisks indicate letters included in the appendix to this book.[12]

---

in antiquity that the letter of Nicias (Th. 7 11-15) and those of Demosthenes were rhetorically stylized. Dion. Hal. treated such letters as oratory in *Th.* (42) and *Dem.* (23). Demetr. *de Eloc.* (228) called them treaties (*syggrammata*) with greeting (*chairein*) attached. For Demosthenes see Jonathan A. Goldstein, *The Letters of Demosthenes* (New York and London: Columbia University Press, 1968). Goldstein supports the genuineness of D. *Epp.* 1-4 by his rhetorical analyses. He adds, "Hence, if the author uses the style and locutions of an oration rather than those of a letter, there is no reason to think that he forgot that he was writing and not speaking, and still less to suspect the document of inauthenticity" (99). See his section, "The Rhetorical Analysis of the Letters," 133-81.

11. Rhetorical style in the example letters of Hellenistic correspondence is limited to choice of words and turn of phrases. The subject matter, usually one chief message, limited the style of executive orders. For Welles' classification of the royal letters see *Royal Cor.,* "The Composition and Style of the Letters," xli-l, and his commentary on each letter. His summary statement reads, ". . . it is clear that the official letter like the private letter was evolved first as a purely practical instrument of communication. Its development was as far as can be determined uninfluenced by the rhetorical schools" (xlii). The official letter to an individual "was originally in form a private letter; the official letter to a community was based on the prevailing form of communication between communities, the city decree" (xlii-xliii). The prevalence of the personal letter in daily life has influenced the official. For the early origin of the personal out of the official see M. Luther Stirewalt, *Studies in Ancient Greek Epistolography,* SBLRBS 27 (Atlanta: Scholars Press, 1993), 6-10. For the dialogical nature of Paul's letters see Chap. IV, p. 111.

12. References are to Welles, *Royal Cor.;* Sherk, *Roman Documents* (above, note 5); P. Viereck, *Sermo Graecus quo Senatus Populusque Romanus Magistratusque Populi Romani usque ad Tiberii Caesaris Aetatem in Scriptis Publicis Usi Sunt Examinatur* (Göttingen, 1888).

I. Reports to a constituted body:

    A. from ambassadors, special envoys: J. *Life* 217 (in text below); see Aesch. *Or.* 2 128-29.

    B. from military officers: Nicias' letter, Th. 7 11-15; J. *J.W.* 3 138-40; cf. *Life* 62 (no texts given).

    C. from prominent public citizens (below, III A).

II. Executive or administrative:

    A. those conveying orders, decisions, commendations, reports, to a subject community or representatives thereof,

        1. from the highest authority, the royal letters,

            a. regarding business originating with the king: Welles, no. 14* (see below); Letter of Philip (D. *Or.* 12).

            b. regarding business originating with subjects to which the king responds to communities: Welles, nos. 25; 31-32; or to individuals (C. below).

        2. from officials of high station whose authority is granted and sanctioned by a higher authority: Sherk, nos. 34*, 35*.

    B. those conveying orders, decisions, from a constituted body to a military officer or an ambassador in the field: J. *Life* 216-18*.

    C. to or among individuals,

        1. from king to individuals: Welles, no. 58* (see below).

        2. among officials: J. *Life* 226-27.*

    D. communications between states (fictitious letters): Philip, D. *Or.* 18 *(De Corona)* 39*; Sparta to the Jews, 1 Macc 14:20b-23.

III. The reverse line of communicating, i.e. from a private citizen to public officials,

    A. Demosthenes to the Assembly: D. *Epp.* 1-4 (see below).

    B. petitions: White, *Petition,* no. 21 *et alia.*

In view of the vast field and in order to illustrate the influence of the official letter on Paul's letter writing, the types are prioritized and the significance of lesser types accordingly reduced. The letters of the Hellenistic kings and those of similar form written by Roman officials (that is, those of the second class) are given priority because of their wide influence. These letters will, therefore, provide the first examples of the forms and formulae found also in Paul's letters. A second source is provided by letters to and from lesser officials, chiefly from the papyri. The more peripheral letters of the third source are gleaned for supportive evidence and to illustrate certain commonly occurring characteristics. In this group are the letters from citizens to officials and the fictitious letters. When a characteristic of form or function is recurrent and is identified both in the secular and in the Pauline letters the evidence is presented. Only selected major characteristics are considered:[13]

1. Salutation:
   a. identification of the primary sender
   b. naming of co-senders
   c. address to multiple recipients.
2. Body:
   a. background (sometimes divided into past and present)
   b. basis or explanation for the message
   c. message: order, request, commendation
   d. promise.
3. Subscription.

C. Official Letters and the Pauline Letters

1. Salutation

Of the official conventions appropriated by Paul the salutation is most distinguishing. It marks the letter as being of the official type. It intro-

---

13. Other similarities between official letters and Paul may be noted. For example, both the spoken letter and the Pauline letters use direct address to the recipients within the letter. Paul, like Demosthenes and others, addresses his hearers throughout the letters. Thucydides does not record a salutation on Nicias' letter, but has him address the Athenians in the opening sentence and throughout. For personal letters see Chap. I, "Logistics," notes 18 and 19.

duces the writer as one who occupies an authoritative position and identifies the recipients as a corporate body for which the writer is an authority. The recipients would have immediately recognized the nature of the letter, the position of the writer, and their own position in relation to him. Therefore salutations receive special attention here. The body requires less notice; its divisions are of less significance for determining type. The major divisions, background and message(s), are common elements in the bodies (subjects) of most forms of logical communications both oral and written. However, certain units within the letters and the subscriptions reveal an epistolary sub-letter form that demonstrates Paul's preoccupation with the letter-form in the composition of his communications.

a. Identification of Principal Sender

The full identification of the writer in personal familial letters is hardly necessary.[14] In personal business letters a partial designation may be given depending on the circumstances.[15] Lesser bureaucrats also used only partial identification.[16] In royal letters the king, who was the high-

---

14. The writer of a letter to Zenon complaining about mistreatment of her son does well to identify herself: "Simale, mother of Herophantos. . . ." *PCol* III 6 (257 BCE) = White, *Light*, no. 10.

15. In an agreement with contractors Irene and her guardian husband are fully identified. *PMich* III 183 (182 BCE) = no. 30 in White, *Light.** As White notes, this is a legal agreement in letter form. Full identity is required in legal documents. See the collection in K & W, nos. 82-120. For a personal business letter in intimate terms see below, note 27.

16. *PTebt* 289 (23 CE) = K & W, no. 76; *PTebt* 48 (ca. 113 BCE) = K & W, no. 73; *PGiss* 11 (118 CE) = K & W, no. 78, J. *Ant.* 12 45; 51. *Kratistos* was sufficient for some Egyptian officials, e.g. *POxy* 2107; and Chief Physician in *SelPap* I 104 (1 BCE) = White, *Light*, no. 61. In papyri official letters the patronymic is usually omitted: *POxy* 1409; 2105; 2108; 2109; 1423. See the long list of titles in *POslo* 85. For wide variety in identification of the sender in Hebrew letters see Dennis Pardee, "An Overview of Ancient Hebrew Epistolography," *JBL* 97 (1978): 336-37. Pardee writes (p. 337): "At the time of Bar Kokhba, however, self-identification by the sender was apparently mandatory since all of that correspondence contains, where intact, the name(s) of the sender(s) (*papMur* 42, 43, 44, 46; 5/6 *Hev* 7,12) and once, in addition to the names, an epithet (*papMur* 42, 'the village managers of Beth Mashko')." Also circular letters from chief rabbis need no sender identification. See the examples in Jacob Neusner, *A Life of Rabban Yohanan ben Zakkai ca. 1-80 C.E.* (Leiden: Brill, 1962), 41-43; Taatz, *Frühjüdische Briefe* (above, note 8), 82-89. Hugo Mantel lists the uses of the pastoral letter by rabbis (*Studies in the History of the Sanhedrin* [Cambridge, MA: Harvard University Press, 1961], 190-95).

est ranking official and who was served by a highly efficient chancery and envoys, used only his title but may also have added a farewell.[17] In these cases the relationship, status, or line of authority needed no notice or emphasis.

To the other extent, the sender was fully identified in three types of letters that were widely diverse in setting. One was used by Roman emperors who gave themselves full identification. These are understandably of limited use and need no further notice.[18] Another type was written by citizens petitioning for official action. The third type was written by those who held a high office, who were responsible to a higher official, and who addressed a jurisdiction under their authority; these are worthy of special notice. The heading on a letter sent by a Roman strategus to Teos runs as follows:

> Marcus Valerius, son of Marcus, strategus, [the] tribunes and the senate to the council and people of Teos greeting. (Sherk, no. 34*)

A similar example specifies the sender's nationality:

> Lucius Cornelius Scipio, consul of the Romans, and Publius Scipio, brother, to the Council and people of the Heracleans greetings. (Sherk, no. 35*[19])

The units identifying the principal sender of each letter are his name, his patronymic, his title, and his nationality (in the second example).

Full sender identification was also a distinguishing mark of letters of petition. In these letters from private citizens to officials the writer

17. That the king may have added the farewell in his own hand, see Welles, *Royal Cor.,* xxxix.

18. E.g. "Emperor Caesar Augustus, son of the deified [Julius], pontifex maximus, consul-designate for the twelfth time, and holding the tribunician power for the eighteenth time, to the magistrates, the Senate, the people of Cnidos, greetings." No. 147 in Allan Chester Johnson et al., *Ancient Roman Statutes: A Translation with Introduction, Commentary, Glossary, and Index* (Austin: University of Texas Press, 1961) = Sherk, *Roman Documents,* no. 67. Such headings are henceforth disregarded as being atypical.

19. Note, A and A' (co-senders) to B (multiple/corporate recipients). See also Sherk, nos. 38, 43, Viereck, no. V. National representation seems to be often taken for granted; it is omitted in Sherk, nos. 4, 18, 21, 28, 49, 55. The patronymic is omitted in nos. 33, 35, 36. Only the sender's name appears on nos. 5, 48, 63. I have not determined a rationale behind these differences.

had to clearly describe his person and location. John White provides an excellent example, complete with structural analysis:

opening formulaic address (to B from A):
To Aesclepiades, king's cousin [an honorary title] and
strategus, from Dionysius

lineage item:
son of Cephales

vocation item:
cultivator of Crown land

residence item:
of the village of Tenis also called Akoris in the Mochite district.[20]

Two uses of the sender's full identification are shown in these examples. The one is a Roman strategus who is responsible to a superior authority but who also presides over a political jurisdiction. His national office suffices as a residence item; its physical location is certainly well known. His personal identity and his official position define the basis of his authority. He is an intermediary link in the political order.[21] The other is a petition making an appeal as a commoner to a ranking official. The writer concedes his subordinate position by using

20. *PRein* 18 (108 BCE); no. 14* in John L. White, *The Form and Structure of the Official Petition: A Study in Greek Epistolography*, SBLDS 5 (Missoula, MT: Scholars Press, 1972); hereafter = White, *Petition;* see p. 14. There was no mistaking Sentheus. He uses his patronymic and names his village then adds that he dwells "in the sandy quarter of the farmstead [of two people named]." His signature at the end reads: "Sentheus, aged 30 years, with a scar on his left wrist." *Ibid.*, no. 19 (29 CE). See the need of a Jewish inhabitant of Alexandria to give his full identification: White, *Light*, no. 86. The initial address, "To B from A," is regularly employed in petitions; see White, "The Greek Documentary Tradition Third Century B.C.E. to Third Century C.E.," in John L. White (ed.), *Studies in Ancient Letter Writing*, Semeia 22 (Chico, CA: Scholars Press, 1982), 94 (2.12).

21. The intermediary service by a deputy is sometimes noted, e.g. *POxy* 2114 (316 CE) = K & W, no. 81: "Aurelius Apollonius also called Eudaemon, strategus of the Oxyrhynchite nome, through his deputy Plu . . . , to his dearest Aurelius Heras, *praepositus* of the 8th pagus, greeting." Cf. *POxy* 2108, lines 16-17: "The Senate of Hermopolis through Aurelius . . . to Aurelius Serapion. . . ." Cf. 1 Peter 5:12.

the salutation "to B from A." He gives personal identity and validates his citizenship in an ascending scale of notations: family, community, name, and division. These specifications make it assured that he will not be confused with someone else and that contact with him can be made directly. These two uses of sender identification — personal identity and authority — serve to authenticate the letter.[22]

Paul's identification of himself as principal sender follows that of the letter from a ranking officer to the people of his jurisdiction. He begins by identifying himself, his co-senders (when necessary), and his recipients. He then adds a vocation item: apostle (1 and 2 Cor, Gal), servant and apostle (Rom), servant (Phil), prisoner (Phlm), and so on. He substitutes a spiritual lineage for a genealogical one, and it follows and modifies the vocational item: "apostle not from men nor through men but through Jesus Christ and God the Father" (Gal), "apostle called by the will of God" (1 and 2 Cor; Eph; Col), "servant of Jesus Christ"[23] (Phil), "prisoner for Jesus Christ" (Phlm). He thus establishes his sender identity using the standards of the official letter, but modifies it to suit his official position in the Christian community.

b. Identification of Co-senders

Paul's letters regularly mention co-senders. Galatians names an anonymous group of brothers. First Corinthians is from Paul and Sosthenes. Only Timothy is named in 2 Corinthians, Philippians, Philemon (Col). Along with Paul and Timothy, Silvanus is included in 1 Thessalonians (and 2 Thess). Romans is an exception (and Eph); only Paul's name appears.

22. Aune says, ". . . the use of epithets [for sender identification] in early Christian letters suggests their function as 'official' correspondence" (David E. Aune, *The New Testament in Its Literary Environment*, Library of Early Christianity 8 [Philadelphia: Westminster, 1987], 184).

23. The "lineage" of a freedman was sometimes expressed by the genitive of the master's name; e.g. White, *Petition* (above, note 20), nos. 36, 56. Cf. the modified identification of Timothy: patronymic, ". . . my beloved and faithful child in the Lord . . ."; vocation, ". . . to remind you of my ways in Christ Jesus . . ." 1 Cor. 4:17. For this verse Funk speaks of introductory formula, credentials clause, purpose clause (Robert W. Funk, "The Apostolic *Parousia*: Form and Significance," in *Christian History and Interpretation: Studies Presented to John Knox*, ed. W. R. Farmer, C. F. D. Moule, and R. R. Niebuhr [Cambridge: Cambridge University Press, 1967], 255).

The persistence of this practice, the repeated use of Timothy's name, the variations in person and number of co-senders, and the omission in Romans all indicate that the practice was customary and a significant Pauline convention, the particular purpose of which was known to the parties concerned but is less apparent today. It is noteworthy that no other reference is made to a co-sender as co-sender; for example Paul never writes, "Timothy and I say . . . ;" or "Timothy and I send greetings." Nothing within the letters explicitly accounts for the additional signatures.

As seen in Chapter I, no evidence identifies Timothy as a carrier, and the available evidence in fact eliminates him from this role.[24] No conclusion can be drawn regarding Sosthenes and Silvanus. Perhaps the three did help to record or formulate the message; or perhaps the latter two served as carriers.[25] In either case, some acknowledgment of their role might be expected. Although a co-sender may have had some limited activity in the preparation and dispatch of a letter, an explanation of this role must be sought beyond a function limited to participation in these adjunct activities.

In secular letter-writing co-senders are named as necessary in the following types of letters: The personal, familial letter usually originates from a single person.[26] The personal business letter comes from co-

24. If Rom 16 was originally part of the letter it is noteworthy that Timothy sends greetings, but neither he nor anyone else is named as co-sender. He is the co-sender of Phil and is highly commended by Paul (2:19-24); but he is not included in the final greetings (4:21-22). He is the co-sender of Phlm but is not listed with the five others who send greetings (23-24). To the contrary, Titus is never named as co-sender but did serve as carrier. See Chap. I, "Logistics," 11-12, and esp. Margaret M. Mitchell, "New Testament Envoys in the Context of Greco-Roman Diplomatic and Epistolary Conventions: The Example of Timothy and Titus," *JBL* 111 (1992): 641-62.

25. Binder thinks that Silvanus composed much of 1 Thess (Hermann Binder, "Paulus und die Thessalonischerbriefe," in Raymond F. Collins [ed.], *The Thessalonian Correspondence* [Leuven: Lueven University Press/Peeters, 1990], 87-91). Hereafter = Collins, *Thess.* Regarding 2 Thess see *ibid.*, 92-93. In Binder's analysis Silvanus seems to be more of an editor with a free hand. E.g. Paul concludes with 3:11-12, and Silvanus adds the eschatological, apocalyptic note in v. 13. Meeks speaks of "coauthors" or "joint author" (Wayne A. Meeks, *The First Urban Christians: The Social World of the Apostle Paul* [New Haven and London: Yale University Press, 1983], 133, 215 note 27, 224 note 69). Hereafter = Meeks, *Urban Christians.* Jerome Murphy O'Connor, *Paul the Letter-Writer: His World, His Options, His Skills* (Collegeville, MN.: The Liturgical Press, 1995). He does not consider official letter writing.

26. Of the fifty personal letters in K & W only one names dual senders, and that one

senders when the occasion requires.[27] Petitions may originate with dual senders;[28] or they may originate from a corporate group of people.[29]

is, in intent, a business letter. See the translation in the next note. Greetings to and from third parties seems to have been the manner in which others participated in the communication.

27. For example, one letter apparently addressed to a trusted steward, with genuine expressions of concern and with familial language, deals only with business. It reads:

> Demarion and Irene to their dearest Syrus, very many greetings. We know that you are distressed about the deficiency of water [. . .] and we hope that with God's help the field will be sown. Put down to our account everything you spend [. . .]. We pray for your health. [Addressed] To Syrus from Irene and Demarion. (*PRyl* 243 = K & W no. 46)

Notice the 1st pers. pl. throughout and the repetition of both names (in reverse order) in the address. It appears that both parties are involved in some contractual agreement. Other personal business letters: *PMich* III 183 = White, *Light* (above, note 5), no. 30; *PFay* 99 = Exler, p. 38; *POxy* 50; 242; 1770, Exler 14, p. 34; see others, *ibid.,* pp. 33-35. Francis X. J. Exler, *The Form of the Ancient Greek Letter: A Study in Greek Epistolography* (Washington, DC: Catholic University of America, 1923).

28. Senders may be named separately. For example, Lucius Valerius Lucretianus and Lucius Longinus Herennius complain about the imposition of a liturgy. The first person plural is used throughout the body of the letter. However, it is signed: "I Lucius Valerius Lucretianus have presented this, and I wrote for Herennius, as he is illiterate." Both parties are involved in the dispute; both are named in the heading and referred to by the plural references in the body. The first named is responsible for the writing and signs both for himself and for the illiterate Herennius. White, *Petition* (above, note 20), no. 59. In other cases the involvement of the parties may be more complicated. Two brothers petition for redress for damage to their grain fields:

> [To the strategus], Mysthes and Pelopion both sons of Pelops. [The dating] as I was making an inspection of the land [. . .] we found that the young wheat and barley which we have on the farm had been grazed down by the sheep of Harmiusis [fully identified], Aunes son of Minches being witness to it [damage estimated]. I therefore request that he be brought before you [. . .]. (White, *Petition* no. 23*)

There is no signature of sender or scribe at the end, only farewell. The situation seems to be that Mysthes discovered the damage and composed the letter. His brother was not with him at the time but another person, Aunes, was with him and so served as a witness. Nevertheless both owners of the field must be named in the heading. Cf. *ibid.,* nos. 23 (31 CE), 59 (196 CE).

29. E.g. from White, *Petition* (above, note 20). Five cultivators of crown land regarding a litigation, no. 9 (*PAmh* 33, ca. 157 CE); 6 collectors of poll tax regarding their jobs,

In the royal letters the scribes of the chancery were in effect co-senders even though only the king is named in the salutation. Epistolographers drafted and even composed letters. For letter no. 58* Welles
could say, "[It] is nothing more but a form . . . a collection of chancery
phrases."[30] The scribes functioned as co-senders by participating in the
letter's production, and by keeping the archives they could at any time
confirm the letter-event.

On the other hand, high-ranking intermediary officials customarily included in the salutation the governing body to which they were
responsible,

> Marcus Valerius . . . and the senate to the council and people of Teos
> greeting. (Sherk, no. 34* = Viereck, no. II; cf. Sherk, no. 43 =
> Viereck, no. IV[31])
> Jonathan and the Gerousia. . . . (1 Macc 12:6; cf. J. *Ant.* 13 166)
> The brethren, both the apostles and the elders, the brethren who
> are of the Gentiles. . . . (Acts 15:23)

Members of an accompanying or visiting embassy are recognized by
being included as co-senders:

> Gaius Manlius . . . and the emissaries from Rome to the Council
> and people of Heracleia greeting. (Sherk, no. 35*[32])
> Jonathan and those with him who have been sent from Jerusalem to
> Josephus, greeting. (Cf. 226 *Vita* 217; 228)

---

no. 47 (*PGraux* 2, 50-55 CE); 25 villagers regarding trouble over shore land, no. 61 (*PGren*
16, 207 CE); priests regarding rent from temple land, no. 11 (*PAmh* 35, 132 CE); three agents,
collectors of bread for the military, forward a receipt to be signed (*POxy* 1115, 284 CE = K
& W, no. 80).

30. For the work of the chancery see Welles, *Royal Cor.,* xxxvii-xxxviii. For the
Romans: Fergus Millar, "Emperors at Work," *JRS* 57 (1967): 9-19. Some subscriptions explicitly authenticate a letter. See "Subscriptions" below.

31. Co-senders may be two high-ranking intermediary officials. E.g., Scipio and his
brother are co-senders of a letter to Colophon (Sherk, no. 36); and two consuls send a
letter (*ibid.,* no. 61). Cf. Sherk, *Roman Documents,* nos. 5, 23, 35*, 38, 39.

32. A delegation of nine Pergamene citizens met with the governor of Asia to discuss
asylum and the sacred laws of the temple of Asclepius. Sherk, *Roman Documents,* no. 55
(46-44 BCE).

Paul an apostle . . . and the whole emissary with me to the churches
of Galatia. . . . (Gal 1:1[33])

Also in letters between lesser officials, co-senders are customarily
named. They are sometimes colleagues — fellow officials in the secular
world, fellow priests in the religious world. Thus from the secular
world:

To Menches, komogrammateus of Kerkeosiris, from Horus,
komark and the elders of the cultivators of the said village. (*PTebt*
48, K & W, no. 73 [ca. 113 BCE][34])

And from the religious world:

To Serenus, royal scribe [. . . from several priests by name, the text
is fragmented] and the other priests of the same temple, greeting.
(*PIand* 34 [ca. 190 CE])

From Simeon ben Gamaliel and from Yohanan ben Zakkai, to our
brothers. . . . Peace! Let it be known to you. . . .[35]

In summary, then, co-senders are named in the following instances:

1. among family and friends only occasionally when a co-sender is
   drawn into the circle.
2. on personal business as the transaction requires.
3. from citizens to officials:
   a. as partners when equally involved in the matter; or one party
      may take the responsibility and represent the others; or a

---

33. See Chap. III, "The Letters." Cf. J. *Life* 226; Polycarp *Phil.;* Ps. Ignatius to John
Evangelist.

34. The letter is a petition for redress after an assault while the men were perform-
ing their duties. See those from a komarch and elders: K & W, no. 74 = *PTebt* 22 (112 BCE);
no. 73 (113 BCE); *PTebt* 907: "Pasis, Komark of Oxyrhynchus and the *presbyteroi* of farmers
to Typho and the guards with him, greeting."

35. J. Neusner, *Life of Rabban Yohanan* (above, note 16), 41-42. See also Acts 15:23
quoted above; Arthur Cowley, *Aramaic Papyri of the Fifth Century B.C.* (Oxford: Clarendon
Press, 1923; reprint, Osnabruck: O. Zeller, 1967), nos. 30, 31; Sanh. 11a, b; note the phrase
within the body: "It seems advisable to me and to my colleague [. . .]." Taatz, *Frühjüdische
Briefe* (above, note 8), "Rabbinische Briefe," 82-89.

group may write as a unit without designating a representative.

4. from official to official:
   a. as a multiple, silent confirmation and a sharing of authority when two or more colleagues send an order, request, or decision.
   b. as an official representative of a group.
5. from intermediary official to a jurisdiction:
   a. as a courteous reminder when a high ranking official names his governing body and thereby transmits their authority through him to the recipients.
   b. as a courtesy when a high ranking official includes an accompanying embassy and thereby shares authority with them.
6. from king and chancery.

From this overview it is clear that when co-senders are named, they are named for two somewhat different purposes. When an official's superior body is named, the chain of authority and the writer's position are identified. When other individuals or colleagues are named, the writer shares with these persons the authority and responsibility. In the latter case the co-sender is at least a silent witness to the letter's preparation and content and at most a legal witness or notary to the message.

Having only impermanent and intangible bases, Paul names individual co-senders as his supporting base. These temporary scribes and supporters took the place of an official chancery or governing body, witnessing to the letter-event. This was a necessary convention in his world of communication, a convention used also by secular officials in similar positions. His practice of naming co-senders is, therefore, most similar to that which includes colleagues, fellow officials or priests, or, in the case of Galatians, an embassy present with him. Paul acknowledges his authority and its derivation from Christ, but he also shares responsibility and secures witnesses to the epistolary event and the message.

This interpretation of the function of Pauline co-senders is supported by the essential requirement of witnessing in Jewish and Christian societies. Two or three witnesses to oral presentations were consistently required in the early church and the same standard had long been applied to letter writing in Jewish society. The foremost example of Jewish witness to written documents must be the Bar Kokhba letter. It was written by two officials at Bet Mashko to a military officer on behalf of a citizen to confirm and witness his purchase of a cow and to secure its safe transportation. The names of two co-senders appear at the beginning and are repeated at the end as those who wrote (dictated) the letter. The man who sold the cow confirms the transaction. Two witnesses are named, along with an attestant (one who "causes to testify") — that is, the scribe or a notary.[36] In an Aramaic papyrus the identity of multiple senders, "Yedoniah and his colleagues, the priests," is repeated after a health prayer as introduction to a narrative background and again to introduce a request with the additional phrase, "and the Jews all [of them] inhabitants of Yeb say as follows: . . ."[37] And William L. Holladay says of Jeremiah's Letter (Chap. 29), "'Verse 23b 'I am witness,' functions in two ways. First . . . 'witness' denotes a counter-signatory for the letter [by Jeremiah]. . . . The letter in the present passage is a letter from [Jeremiah] to the exiles (v 1), but it also sets itself forth as a message from Yahweh . . . , so this phrase is the equivalent of 'countersigned, Yahweh.'"[38]

Paul was well acquainted with the requirement for witnesses. He was represented by Titus at Corinth for the collection of the Relief Fund (2 Cor 8:16), and by "our brother" (v. 22); these two appear to be accountable to and for Paul. A third member on the committee had been "appointed by the churches" and was accountable to them (v. 19).

In the same letter Paul uses dual witness in quite a different situation. He wrote to the Corinthians,

> Nevertheless (you say) since I was crafty, I took you in by deceit.
> Did I take advantage of you by any I sent to you? I urged Titus to

36. Dennis Pardee, "An Overview of Ancient Hebrew Epistolography" (above, note 16), 341; and the literature. For the Greek practice, Schnider and Stenger emphasize the shared authority of co-senders (*Studien* [above, note 9]), 4. Shared authority in turn implies shared responsibility. See also Victor Paul Furnish, *II Corinthians*, The Anchor Bible (Garden City, NY: Doubleday, 1984), 103-4.

37. No. 30 in Cowley, *Aramaic Papyri*.

38. William L. Holladay, *Jeremiah 2* (Philadelphia: Fortress, 1989), "A Letter to the Exiles," 131-44; quotation from p. 139. Also, J. Jeremias, "Paarweise Sendung in Neuen Testament," in A. J. B. Higgins (ed.), *New Testament Essays: Studies in Memory of Thomas Walter Manson* (Manchester: Manchester University Press, 1959), 136-43; Jeremias, *New Testament Theology* (New York: Scribners, 1971), 235.

go and sent the brother with him. Titus did not take advantage of you, did he? (2 Cor 12:16b-18a)

The implication of this dialogue is clear. If the Corinthians were to accuse Titus of taking advantage of them, Paul subtly reminds them that there was another witness to the occasion, the brother. And he warns the people shortly thereafter, "This is the third time I am coming to you. Any charge must be sustained by the evidence of two or three witnesses" (2 Cor 13:1; cf. Deut 19:15).

In the decision from the Jerusalem Council (Acts 15) the multiple witnesses are, first, the two groups of senders, the apostles and the elders; and second, they in turn are represented by two pairs of messengers, Judas Barsabbas and Silas, Paul and Barnabas. This compound witnessing identifies the line of authority and validates the message epitomized in the letter (vv. 22-29). It also authenticates the mission and corroborates the oral reports that the two pairs of messengers will give.

In conclusion and without explicit explanation of the function of co-senders, a function may be deduced from this survey. A convincing accounting for the use both by Paul and by the secular writers is to identify co-senders as personnel who were informed participants in the letter-event and who supplied the requirements for witness to the written message. Thus Timothy, Sosthenes, and Silvanus could at any time authenticate a letter, its origin, and its content. In fact Timothy's role in the troubles at Corinth was to remind the people of Paul's teachings (1 Cor 4:17). Under this general assignment he was present both to confirm a correction to a misinterpretation of a previous letter and to verify Paul's restatement of it in the present letter (1 Cor 5:9-13).

c. Address to Multiple Recipients

The personal letter is customarily addressed to one recipient; occasionally other family members or friends are named.[39] In personal corre-

---

39. E.g. Esthladas to his father and mother, *WChrest* 10 = K & W, no. 33 (130 BCE); consolation to friends *POxy* 115 (ii CE); Plato *Epp.* 6, 13; Isoc. *Epp.* 4, 5; D. *Ep.* 5. The address on Plato *Epp.* 7 and 8, "Plato to the friends and followers of Dion," marks them as other than personal letters.

spondence recognition of other people in the recipient community is usually made through the exchange of greetings at the end of the letter.

The administrative letter, on the other hand, is frequently directed to multiple recipients who are often addressed as a community. For example, royal letters in response to petitions from cities[40] and those from high ranking officials in charge of a jurisdiction (see the model letters in the Appendix) are addressed to an administrative body and to the people.[41] A commander-in-chief might address the whole army from officers to infantry.[42] Among lesser bureaucrats the address is multiple when the occasion requires; thus a dioicetes writes a circular letter to be sent to responsible officials concerning the dikes of the Nile.[43]

Multiple address in official communication is, therefore, used to disseminate an order or directive, to publicize announcements, and to indicate that the business at hand dealt with public and not private

40. Welles, *Royal Cor.*, nos. 2, 4, 6, 15, 22, 25, 31, 34, 35, 62; no. 56 bypasses the city and addresses only the governor; no. 52 is addressed, "to the league of the Ionians."

41. Sherk's collection shows combinations of multiple addressees as the occasion demanded: magistrates, council, senate, city, people; most often to magistrates *(archousi)*, council *(boulei)*, people *(dēmoi)*, *Roman Documents*, nos. 18, 20, 21, 23, 26, 28, 49, 55. Also 1 Macc 13:36; 15:2b; 11:30; J. *Ant.* 13 126; 1 Kgs 21:8; 2 Kgs 19:1; Jer. 29:1, 4, 24-25; Cowley, *Aramaic Papyri,* no. 30 (lines 17b-19a); D. *Or.* 18 *(de Corona)* 39* (a fictitious letter of Philip). Goldstein notes that the *demogoria* type of spoken letters is customarily addressed to council and people (Goldstein, *Demosthenes* [above, note 10], 100-102). Sherk, no. 63 (324), is addressed to a *gerousia* "an aristocratic corporation of elder citizens . . . concerned with the management of one or two of the local cults."

42. Welles, *Royal Cor.*, no. 39 (ca. 203 BCE), "King Antiochus to generals, cavalry and infantry officers, soldiers, and the rest, greetings." Note *ad loc.:* "This, except for *tois allois,* is an ordinary heading of a general order to the army." Also Welles, no. 16; 1 Macc 7:1; 14:16; 3 Macc 3:12; J. *J.W.* 1 667. See the other inclusive phrases in some headings: 3 Macc 3:12; *Martyrdom of Polycarp;* Cowley, *Aramaic Papyri,* nos. 38, 30.

43. *POxy* 1409. The dioicetes was the minister of finance ". . . who was responsible for the collection of revenues . . ." (K & W, p. 3). Cf. K & W, nos. 85, 86. Letters circulated among separated recipients were used when the occasion required. Welles, *Royal Cor.,* no. 1, is from Antigonus to Scepsis. It appears to be a copy of a circular to be sent among the Greek cities. Welles remarks (p. 11), "Nothing, except the heading and the name of the envoy at the end, need have been changed before it could have been sent to any other Greek city." It is an historical, autobiographical account which covers 68 of the 72 remaining lines. See the comparison of this letter with Galatians in Chap. III. Other nearly autobiographic narratives: Welles, nos. 14, 52; in 52 Eumenes II records at length the honors granted him by the Ionian League.

matters. It recognizes that the recipients form a definable or constituted body, the members of which receive and hear the communication
and thereby share the responsibility of compliance or share an honor
or commendation.

With one exception, Paul uses the multiple address, and it serves a
purpose similar to that used by officials to address a jurisdiction. He
consistently addresses an ecclesia, an organized body of believers. He
addresses only the ecclesia (1 Thess); the ecclesia and officers (Phil); the
local ecclesia and saints in general (1 Cor); the local ecclesia and the
saints in Achaia (2 Cor);[44] the ecclesiae in Galatia; three individuals and
the ecclesia (Phlm). The exception is the generalized address to the
Romans, "to all God's beloved in Rome."

It is worth noting briefly that Paul owed something of the tone of
his address to the personal letter. He wrote with familiarity and often
tenderness; note his repeated use of "beloved" and *"adelphoi."*[45] But this
warmth was conveyed within an adaptation of the official convention;
sender, co-sender, and recipients are all identified using forms that parallel those used by ranking officials to the people of their jurisdictions.

2. Body

As noted above, the salutation is the unit that identifies the genre of
any given letter. But most official letters also share a twofold body
structure, consisting of background information and a message. The
background may be a short notification or reminder, or it may be a
more official recording of previous events or transactions.[46] The message, in turn, for which the background prepares the way, conveys an
order, request, or announcement. At times a basis or explanation of the
decision and a promise (or threat) is added to the message. This letter-
form is extremely widespread, common in the royal letters, letters of in-

---

44. For the salutation on 1 and 2 Cor see Chap. III, "The Letters," 78-80.

45. For friendship language in Paul's letters, see Chap. III, "The Letters," section on
Philippians, 84-91.

46. Of course in personal letters the writer may give an introductory sentence by
way of reminder or preface. It has little of the function of the background of the official
letter. For a kind of background and request pattern and formulae see White, "Documentary Letter Tradition" (above, note 20), 95-100 (2.2–2.33).

termediary officials, letters from Egyptian officials, and those that can be garnered from Gentile and Jewish documents and literary works and petitions. A composite list of major body characteristics includes:[47]

1. background;
2. basis or explanation for the message (decision);
3. message;
4. promise or threat.[48]

The chief characteristics of the official letter-body are evident in Paul's letters; he adopts the natural twofold structure. However, as already seen in the other units of his letters, his letter-bodies also transcend stereotypic patterns. Into the two divisions he incorporates personal history, biography, apology, defense. He also introduces excursuses and illustrations and metaphors as they come to mind, and does it all in epistolary and/or rhetorical expressions as they fit his thought and mood. The influence of official letter writing on the bodies of Paul's letters is demonstrated in Chapter III, and the letters in the Appendix are arranged to show the units of the body.[49]

---

47. Other units would include transition sentences, disclosure formulae, concluding instructions, and the like. For a listing and selected literature see James L. Bailey and Lyle D. Vander Broek, *Literary Forms in the New Testament: A Handbook* (Louisville: Westminster/John Knox, 1992), 25-27. Although based chiefly on personal letters, White's analysis of the body of nonliterary papyri offers a pattern for a more detailed study of the official letter-body under the thesis of this chapter (John L. White, *The Form and Function of the Body of the Greek Letter: A Study of the Letter-Body in the Non-Literary Papyri and in Paul the Apostle*, SBLDS 2 [1972]).

48. For basis or explanation of the message see the model letters and Welles, *Royal Cor.,* nos. 1, 23, 31, 54, 58, 64-67, 71. No. 35 grants a request from Teos; about half of the letter gives three reasons for the compliance. Cf. J. *Ant.* 126-29; Sherk, *Roman Documents,* no. 43 = Viereck, no. IV; 1 Macc 15:16-21; 2 Macc 9:19-27. For promise see Welles, no. 1: "In the future also we shall try to provide for you and for the other Greeks whatever advantage we have in our power" (*Royal Cor.,* lines 67-69). Cf. no. 14*; Sherk, no. 26, lines 22-25. Promise in Paul is expressed by the future tense in benedictions or similar verses: 2 Cor 9:11, "You will be enriched in every way . . ."; 13:11, ". . . and the God of love and peace will be with you." Cf. Phil 4:7, 9, 19-20; 1 Thess 5:24; and note on Phlm under "Subscriptions." The references are gathered by Leonard George Champion, *Benedictions and Doxologies in the Epistles of Paul* (Oxford: Oxford University Press, 1934), 13-17.

49. Welles recognizes the background sections. He says regarding no. 13, "In conformity with epistolary theory it consists of two parts, the information and the order" (*Royal*

3. Sub-letter Forms in Subscriptions and Other Units

In the subscriptions and in other units the letter-form is discernible. They include a modified salutation, body, greeting, and farewell, and are known as sub-letter forms. Neither an afterthought nor a post-script, a subscription is a notation intentionally withheld to the end of a letter by the sender for purposes explored below.[50]

Cor., p. 71; cf. no. 14 and p. 77). No. 18 concerns the sale of real estate; it gives (1) information about the sale, and (2) an order to sell. Even in the more personal of the letters the background provides an official record. Nos. 55-61 are addressed to a priest; ". . . they are personal letters, full of energy and vitality, rapid, colloquial, vivid" (p. 251). In no. 61 the minutes of a conference between King Attalus and his advisers forms the background. The discussion between them is summarized and the opposition of a certain Chlorus is recorded. No. 71 is a personal letter sent from one king to another. See the comparison of no. 1 with Gal, Chap III. No. 7 is a review of arguments of two delegations (only one is preserved). Such reviews of envoys' presentations are minuted backgrounds; e.g., the review of the envoys' presentation of a decree and honors for Artemis, nos. 31-32. No. 31 ". . . is the stock chancery form of the reply to an embassy (Intro., p. xiv)." No. 52: lengthy restatement of a decree granting honors, and the king's acceptance of the honors including his decision concerning the particulars. (Cf. Claudius to the Alexandrians: White, *Light* [above, note 15], no. 88.) No. 75, a semi-biographical review of a city treasurer's service, is background for forgiving him for a minor infraction of the law regarding consecutive terms in office. In some cases a specific order follows the decision forming a tripartite structure; e.g., Welles, *Royal Cor.,* nos. 36, 65. For the dual structure see also D. *Letter* 2: salutation: section 1; theme: 1-2; body: the past 3-12, the present 13-15; request: 16-20; closing: 21-26; farewell. Letter of Nicias (T. 7 11-15): introduction: 11 *init.;* background: the perilous situation of the army in Sicily, 11-14; request, recommendation, conclusion: "'recall the army or replace it,'" 15. Philip's Letter (D. *Or.* 12): background: 1-23a; decision: 23b. The background is a lengthy narrative of recent history. Cowley, *Aramaic Papyr,* no. 30, a description of the conditions in Elephantine; and the description of a letter in D. *Or.* 23 160-61 *et passim,* much of which could be reconstructed.

50. See the true subscriptions on Soc. *Ep.* 28; *PSI* 299 (iii CE = Hunt and Edgar, no. 158); K & W, no. 36 (*POxy* 1481, ii CE); 42 (*PLond* Inv 1575), "Remember our pigeons." There is a type of subscription added by the recipient, i.e. docketing. For this type and for definition see Gordon J. Bahr, "The Subscriptions in the Pauline Letters," *JBL* 87 (1968): 27-41. Bahr's analysis of the point in a letter at which the subscription began is suggestive, but his assumption that a scribe composed much of the body is doubtful. Anticipation of public reading and the rhetorical and animated style suggest dictation, not ghost writing. Dio Chrysostom wrote, "Dictate your writing. It's more like one addressing an audience." D. Chr. 18 18 (LCL II 229). For postscripts see Schnider and Stenger (above, note 9), "Das Postskript," 108-67; Doty's analysis of the letter closings, William G. Doty, *Letters in Primitive Christianity* (Philadelphia: Fortress, 1973), 39-42.

The single word, farewell *(errōso)*, is often the only formal closing of a letter. In other cases the closing is a short sign-off: "I must close now." But when the farewell is written in a second hand it is in itself also a short subscription, usually indicating that a scribe has written the text and the sender is adding the farewell in his own hand. In the personal letter the sender's subscription approves the message and identifies the letter as a token of the self sent as a gift. In the personal business letter it confirms the transaction. In both cases the scribe acts when necessary as a notary for an illiterate.[51] Welles is of the opinion that in the royal letters the king added the farewell in his own hand.[52]

In administrative correspondence among officials the subscription is written to confirm the message. For example, two retiring komarchs write to certify their successor. At the letter's end the scribe "notarizes" the certification in his own hand.[53] Then a farewell is added in a second

---

51. As a personal token Stowers cites (secondhand) *SB* 4 7335, "I pray for your health continually together with that of your children. Farewell" (Stanley K. Stowers, *Letter Writing in Greco-Roman Antiquity* [Philadelphia: Westminster, 1986], 61); cf. *POxy* 3067, p. 72. A guardian husband confirms a transaction for his wife. The subscription in a second hand reads, "I agree to the above written statements" (White, *Light* [above, note 15, no. 30]). The confirmation for an illiterate occurs often; e.g. "I, Aurelius Xanthippus son of Theotecnus, of the Athenaean tribe and the Salaminian deme, wrote for her, as she is illiterate" (*PSI* 1067 [235-37 CE] = K & W, no. 90; cf. 94, 98). White observes concerning the illiteracy formula, ". . . this convention is not employed in ordinary private correspondence, but in official letters or in legal documents" (White, "Documentary Letter Tradition" [above, note 20], 95). For summary and additional references see Bahr, "Subscriptions" (preceding note), 28-29 and notes 5-7 (Bahr treats both letters and "records," *hypomemna*. He limits *hypomemna* to documents which require legal authentication [p. 32]); K & W, nos. 82-120; especially no. 116, deed of gift, a document as well subscribed by all parties as is the Bar Kokhba letter (see above); Chan-Hie Kim, *Form and Structure of the Familiar Greek Letter of Recommendation,* SBLDS 4 (1972), no. 76 (*POxy* 1162); *POxy* 65 = K & W, no. 83; *PSI* 784 = K & W, no. 84. For Paul's use of subscriptions for confirmation see Hans Dieter Betz, *Galatians: A Commentary on Paul's Letter to the Churches in Galatia* (Philadelphia: Fortress, 1979), 312; Weiss, *RGG* (1 1912) III 2202: ". . . die Bitten des Paulus haben fast die Charakter einer Beschworung vor Zeugen."

52. Welles, *Royal Cor.,* xxxix. If this were the case the king's signature on the original document authenticated the message. Confirmation rested in the chancery. The combined authority of king and scribes is felt in the contrast between Welles, no. 73, and *POxy* 1423. In the first King Mithridates writes to a satrap ordering the apprehension of a traitor; no explicit confirmation or witness is necessary. The other, an order for the arrest of a runaway slave, is strongly and personally confirmed by the official. See the text above.

53. *PClair Isidor* 125 (308 CE). Bahr writes regarding documents, "The subscription

hand, the sender's, and it is sufficient to authenticate everything the scribe has written. A similar example may be seen in the case of a higher official who sends an order to the irenarchs of the Oxyrhynchite nome.[54]

A full attestation confirms the order for the arrest of a runaway slave. After the salutation, a single sentence comprises the body of the letter. Then follows in a different hand:

> This order is valid, and in answer to the formal question I gave my consent. I, Flavius Ammonas, *officialis* on the staff of the prefect of Egypt, have made this order. (*POxy* 1423)

As observed above, Jewish custom especially required witnesses to both the written and the spoken word. Concerning the Bar Kokhba communications, Dennis Pardee observes that the letters "have two types of concluding formulae: (i) greetings and (ii) identification by signature." The greetings are health wishes and "function as a final 'with all good wishes,' or 'best regards.'"[55] The second formula, identification by signature, is an authentic subscription. It may be the signature of the sender (*PapMur* 42, 43, 46, 48), of a witness (42), or of a notary (42). Pardee continues: "There are two forms of signature which refer to witnessing [. . .], one form used by the sender ('[. . .] PN wrote it'), and one used by the principal concerned party in the letter of attestation, *PapMur* 42 ('[. . .] Yaaqov ben Yehuda upon his "soul"')."[56]

Subscriptions characterize Paul's letters. In four letters he introduces the subscription by a notation of autograph: "by my own hand." In 2 Corinthians the subscript is preceded by the sentence, "So I write these things while I am away from you," thus eliminating the need for a

---

served to make legally binding the agreement which a scribe had cast in an appropriate written form. Since the subscription was, in fact, a summary of the record in the subscriber's own words (or, perhaps, those of his agent), it was as if the subscriber had written the record himself" (Bahr, "Subscriptions" [above, note 50], 29). A subscription concludes a letter from Mark Anthony to the *koinon* of Asia: "I have written [*gegrapha*] to you concerning these matters" (Sherk, *Roman Documents,* no. 57).

54. *POxy* 2107 (262 CE); the letter concerns a person who has neglected to perform an imposed duty. Cf. 1428; 2108; 2114.

55. Dennis Pardee, "An Overview" (above, note 16), 341.

56. *Ibid.* See also Joseph A. Fitzmyer, "Aramaic Epistolography," in John L. White (ed.), *Studies* (above, note 20), 36-37.

repeated notation of autograph.[57] A pattern built on the body sub-form becomes observable in these units. The units are,

1. salutation: a notation of autograph or equivalent
2. body: exhortation, reiteration, request
3. greeting
4. farewell: a benediction.

For example, consider 2 Corinthians 13:11-14:

1. Salutation: "Finally, brothers and sisters, farewell [*chrairete*]." (11a)
2. Body: "Put things in order, listen to my appeal, agree with one another, live in peace; and the God of love and peace will be with you." (11b; note the promise)
3. Greeting: "Greet one another with a holy kiss. All the saints greet you." (12-13)
4. Farewell: "The grace of the Lord Jesus Christ, the love of God and the communion of the Holy Spirit be with all of you." (14)

Similarly in 1 Corinthians 16:21-24:

1. Notation of autograph (and greeting): "I, Paul, write this greeting with my own hand." (21)
2. Statement of major concern, final admonition: "Let anyone be accursed who has no love for the Lord. Our Lord come!" (22)
3. Greeting, here consisting of the whole subscript: "I, Paul, write this greeting. . . ."
4. Farewell: "The grace of the Lord Jesus be with you. My love be with all of you in Christ Jesus. Amen." (23-24)

The formal subscription in Philemon is preceded by a double background and request. Note that the offer of reimbursement (18) anticipates the first message in the subscription proper (19b-21),

---

57. In letters not having the explicit statement Bahr finds evidence of Paul's autograph (Bahr, "Subscriptions" [above, note 50], 27-41). The lack of a notation of autograph and a clear subscription in Philippians tend to show Paul's hand throughout the letter and to emphasize *philophronēsis* as the major intent of the letter. If there is any reiteration of theme, it is the commendation of Epaphras and the acknowledgment of the Philippians' gifts (4:15-20).

1a. background: "So if you consider me your partner," (17a)
1b. request: "welcome him as you would welcome me." (17b)
2a. background: "If he has wronged you in any way, or owes you any-thing" (18a)
2b. request: "charge that to my account." (18b)

Formal subscript:

1. Salutation (notation of autograph): "I, Paul, am writing this with my own hand." (19a)
2. Body:
   - regarding business at hand: "I will repay it. . . ." (19b-21)
   - regarding personal request: "One thing more — prepare a guest room for me. . . ." (22)
3. Greetings. (23-24)
4. Benediction. (25)

For Galatians, the body of the subscription is a full reiteration of the letter's theme — that is, circumcision versus a new creation.[58] Thus,

1. Salutation (notation of autograph): "See what large letters I make when I am writing in my own hand." (6:11)
2. Body:
   - background: Identification of the opponents and their mo-tive. (12-13)
   - basis for decision: Paul's boast of nothing but the cross. (14)
   - the decision: Circumcision is nothing, the new creation, ev-erything. (15-16)
   - request for personal privilege: "From now on, let no one make trouble for me; for I carry the marks of Jesus branded on my body." (17)

58. Cf. Bahr's remark regarding the subscription as ". . . a summary of the record in the subscriber's own words" (above, note 50); and Betz says, "In [Gal] 6:11-18 Paul adds a postscript in his own handwriting. . . . An autographic postscript serves to authenticate the letter, to sum up its main points, or to add concerns which have come to the mind of the sender after the completion of the letter" (Hans Dieter Betz, *Galatians: A Commentary on Paul's Letter to the Churches in Galatia* [Philadelphia: Fortress, 1979], 312). Schnider and Stenger see in the closing signatures a quasi-legal authentication (*Studien* [above, note 9], 131-35).

3. Greeting omitted, as is common in official letters.
4. Benediction. (18)

It is noteworthy that the body of Galatians is enclosed within the salutation as well as the subscription, both of which are in the sub-letter form. They witness to Paul's personal attention to the preparation and to the underlying priority of the epistolary form in his communications. Thus,

> Background statement: "I am astonished that you are so quickly deserting the one who called you in the grace of Christ and are turning to a different gospel — not that there is another gospel, but there are some who are confusing you and want to pervert the gospel of Christ." (1:6-7)

> Decision and order: "But even if we or an angel from heaven should proclaim to you a gospel contrary to what we proclaimed to you, let that one be accursed! As we have said before, so now I repeat, if anyone proclaims a gospel contrary to what you received, let that one be accursed!" (8-9)

> Closing, an ironic comment on the order: "Am I now seeking human approval, or God's approval? Or am I trying to please people? If I were still pleasing people, I would not be a servant of Christ." (10)

Another use of the sub-letter form occurs in the units of the *peri de* ("now concerning") sections of 1 Corinthians. These are analyzed in Chapter III together with a comparison of a secular letter of similar style. An example is given here, 1 Cor 5:9-13:

> 1a. background past: reference to previous, misinterpreted letter: "I wrote to you in my letter not to associate with sexually immoral persons." (9-10)
> 1b. background present: "But now I am writing to you not to associate with anyone . . . who is sexually immoral." (11)
> 2. basis for decision, the role of judgment: "God will judge those outside." (12-13a)
> 3. decision: "Drive out the wicked person from among you." (13b)

It is thus evident that Paul composes subscriptions incorporating modified units of the letter — salutation, body, greeting, and farewell — into a letter-closing. He rejects the laconic form of the personal letter, choosing instead to modify the official one. The principal sender of an official letter used the subscriptions to mark the letter as his own and to confirm that what his scribe had written was accurate. Such authentication was of singular importance for official and for personal business letters. In like manner Paul's subscriptions give his readers notice that he assumes responsibility for the whole letter.

D. Summary

In these five units — identification of primary sender, naming of co-senders, multiple address, dual structure of the body, and subscriptions — Paul adapted the conventions of official correspondence.

Sender-identity discloses an official's position in the political order. The political order in turn vouches for the authority of the office. The authority resides in the established line. Paul sees himself as an intermediary in the divine kingdom.

In official letters, the writer used as co-senders a governing body or representatives thereof, colleagues, or the anonymous epistolographers of the chanceries. Co-senders share in the letter-event and are witnesses to the letter's message. Paul does not name a governing body; there is none. Rather by his spiritual genealogy he acknowledges Christ as his ultimate authority. As for the support of a chancery, he forms an ad hoc secretariat from co-workers and the resident community who aid in the logistics for the communication and support him in general. He remains as an intermediary official between Christ and the people.

Paul's multiple address also served a purpose similar to that of the official who addressed a jurisdiction. The congregation is the corporate group that receives the message and thereby shares the responsibility of compliance or the reward of commendation. On occasion the people are informed of the activities of Paul, his co-workers, their fellow members, and their sister congregations. The network of activity extends Paul's parish, and his inter-congregational stance puts him in a position of authority vis-à-vis the congregations.

As with his free adaptation of other epistolary resources, in using the dual body form Paul disregards limitations in content and length by incorporating into the necessary background and into intended messages a wide variety of other units suitable to his purposes. The dual form is found in whole letters, in subscriptions, and in the *peri de* sections of 1 Corinthians.

Without the backing of a chancery and with much of the letter in the handwriting of a third party, subscriptions were necessary for lesser officials and for personal business letters. They confirmed the writer's identity and authenticated the message. Paul added a further personal touch by composing them in a modified epistolary sub-form: salutation, body, greeting, farewell.

The new and unique epistolary arm of Paul's ministry required innovative approaches for communication. His innovations were made by a creative synthesis of epistolary settings, forms, and conventions available to him, and these were in turn imbued with his own theological convictions.

III

————————————————

The Letters

In this chapter I would like to make additional observations on the official letter-form and settings in the seven letters that are incontestably Paul's. My chronology is based on that of Jürgen Becker, who asserts the priority of 1 Thessalonians and 1 Corinthians.[1] After these early works I sense on Paul's part a sure confidence in his ability to rely on and adapt letter writing to meet his needs.

First Thessalonians and 1 Corinthians reveal Paul's developing facility with the letter. The former shows a certain tentativeness, while the latter takes a common pattern and intersperses excurses in response to specific reports from Corinth. Thereafter each of the remaining letters shows, in addition to confidence in writing, progressively more freedom in communicating with the people. Philippians demonstrates that, even in the midst of enforced separation, deep affection can be expressed in writing. Philemon conveys similar affection to two estranged friends and at the same time subtly insists on their reconciliation; it is a compact and well-wrought blend of the official and personal forms. Galatians, in a far different mood, delivers a self-assured, apostolic directive to errant churches. Romans takes the expansive form of a letter-essay to address a wide audience with a broad vision of past, present, and future.

A number of the letters in this chapter are compared to similar let-

1. Jürgen Becker, *Paul, Apostle to the Gentiles* (Louisville: Westminster/John Knox, 1993), 17-32. See especially the chart on p. 31.

ters, in their form and settings, from the secular world. There are enough similarities to reveal Paul's general acquaintance with the broad field of official letter writing and his freedom in adapting or disregarding the conventions. The identification of the "brothers" in the Galatians salutation is the key to the letter setting. The treatment of Romans is considered as a closure to the ministry in the eastern Mediterranean.

A. 1 Thessalonians

Some time has apparently elapsed between the founding of the church and the writing of the letter — time enough for the reputation of the Thessalonians to spread "everywhere" (1 Thess 1:8; Acts 17:1-9). Paul was concerned about the Thessalonians, so he sent Timothy to check on them. Too distraught to wait at Ephesus for his return, Paul made his way to Athens to intercept him.[2] First Thessalonians and the account in Acts 17 reveal his anxiety while he awaited Timothy's arrival. When Timothy returned with joyful news, Paul made the unusual decision to respond in writing to the reports from the congregation. Two pertinent observations can be made concerning this early letter. First, there is evidence that Paul has not yet realized the full adaptation of the official letter; second, he shows a hesitancy to resort to writing.

An early, partial adaptation of the official form is evident in the units of the salutation of 1 Thessalonians. Paul uses no sender identity in the salutation.[3] Rather, at the conclusion of the review of his ministry at Thessalonica he gives his credentials (2:1-8; esp. vv. 3-4), and they are used to endorse his former ministry in person, not his letter. The first person plurals include Timothy, whose credentials are given (3:1-3), marking him as a trusted emissary. It appears that Paul has not yet felt the need to establish a sender identity in the salutation; he has not as-

---

2. For a review of Paul's ministry at Thessalonica, see Abraham J. Malherbe, *Paul and the Thessalonians: The Philosophic Tradition of Pastoral Care* (Philadelphia: Fortress, 1987), Chap. 3, "Nurturing the Community," 61-94. Luhrmann draws insights from a comparison of 1 Thess and Acts (Dieter Luhrmann, "The Beginnings of the Church in Thessalonica," in David L. Balch, Everett Ferguson, and Wayne A. Meeks [eds.], *Greeks, Romans, and Christians: Essays in Honor of Abraham J. Malherbe* [Minneapolis: Fortress, 1990], 237-49).

3. For more on Paul's sender identity see Chap. II, 34-37.

sumed all responsibility to himself as he does later. He relies, rather, on the confirmation of the two co-senders.

Only in this letter does Paul name two co-senders: Silvanus and Timothy. Timothy was actively involved with the Thessalonian church from its inception. He has, in fact, just come from Thessalonica and, as emissary, has certainly reported in full to Paul. Silvanus, who was also previously involved in the Thessalonian ministry, served as Paul's companion while Timothy was absent. When the three finally came together they formed a small, transitory Christian community, and the two co-senders aided Paul in the letter's production. There is no indication that any larger community of believers was involved in preparing or sending the letter; if this was indeed the case, 1 Thessalonians stands alone among the Pauline letters for being written in such relative isolation. And it thus becomes easier to understand the intimate involvement of Timothy and Silvanus in the letter-event. Their role is indicated and emphasized by the use of the first person plural throughout the thanksgiving and at the beginning of the account of the ministry in Thessalonica (see especially 1:5b).[4]

The designation of recipients is also unique. This is the only letter in which Paul uses the possessive genitive case to identify the assembly. He writes, ". . . to the church of the Thessalonians. . . ." Then he adds, to denote their spiritual origin and location, ". . . in God the Father and the Lord Jesus Christ." The address suggests a kind of congregational polity, further indicated in that no leader or governing group is

---

4. For co-senders see Franz Schnider and Werner Stenger, *Studien zum neutestamentlichen Briefformular* (Leiden: Brill, 1987), 4-7. See above, Chap. II, section b, "Co-senders." Binder argues that Silvanus composed parts of the letter. He finds that while Timothy may have acted as scribe, Paul dictated 15 times and Silvanus 14 times (Hermann Binder, "Paulus und die Thessalonischerbrief," in Raymond F. Collins [ed.], *The Thessalonian Correspondence* [Leuven: Leuven University Press, 1990], 91). Silvanus may have been more of an editor with a free hand. For example, according to Binder Paul dictated 3:11-12 and Silvanus added the eschatological, apocalyptic note in v. 13. For further study of co-senders see E. Randolf Richards, *The Secretary in the Letters of Paul*, WUNT 2:42 (Tübingen: Mohr/Siebeck, 1991), 153-58. Richards limits his survey of letters almost exclusively to personal letters (see pp. 11, 169), and throughout treats Paul's letters in that category. He recognizes his over-dependence on Cicero (p. 13 and note 69). For grammatical person and the autobiographical and paraenetic sections of the letter see George Lyons, *Pauline Autobiography: Toward a New Understanding*, SBLDS 73 (Atlanta: Scholars Press, 1985), 178-82.

named.[5] He does appeal to the people to respect those who labor among them and have charge of them, and continues with admonitions to the people to care for one another and for their spiritual life (5:12-22). He seems to be visualizing the assembly as a whole, as a group within which individuals are equally involved. Similarly, from his end no greetings are sent (though this omission may also indicate that there was no Christian assembly in the place where Paul was writing).

The body of 1 Thessalonians readily falls into (1) background, a review of the ministry in Thessalonica (1:2–3:13); and (2) messages, topics that commend the loving relationships among the people and emphasize former instructions (4:1–5:22). These messages likely respond to reports from Timothy.

The first portion of the body, the background, is intertwined with a recollection of Paul's successful ministry at Thessalonica and expresses deep friendship and a desire to be present with the people (2–3). It is drawn from memories of his own experience there — memories freshened by reports that have spread throughout the region (1:8-10). Chapters 1–3 form a paean of friendship combining thanksgiving, prayer, and longing. They demonstrate Paul's entwining of personal friendship with the message of the gospel. He writes, "So deeply do we care for you that we are determined to share with you not only the gospel of God but also our own selves, because you have become very dear to us" (2:8).[6]

---

5. Gillman notes, "The second person plural is used some 84 times in 1 Thessalonians, thus indicating how strongly the letter is shaped as an address to the readers" (John Gillman, "Paul's *EISODOS:* The Proclaimed and the Proclaimer [1 Thes 2,8]," in Collins, *Thess. Correspondence* [preceding note], 64, note 9). When Paul uses the word "church" without the genitive he twice designates the location geographically, "to the churches of Galatia"; "to all the saints in Christ Jesus who are at Philippi with the bishops and deacons." Note that the address on Phil may be interpreted as directed to council (bishops and deacons) and people (saints). For the address on 1 Thess see Schnider and Stenger, *Briefformular* (preceding note), 20-22. For Paul's multiple address see Chap. II, 44-46.

6. See Johannes Schoon-Jansen, "On the Use of the Elements of Ancient Epistolography in I Thessalonians," in Karl P. Donfried and Johannes Beutler (eds.), *The Thessalonians Debate: Methodical Discord or Methodical Synthesis?* (Grand Rapids: Eerdmans, 2000), 179-93. Schoon-Jansen identifies the expressions of affection in the letter. Gillman also notes how the media extends Paul's presence. He says, "By manifesting his apostolic presence through emissary and letter he continued to share with them his 'very

Expressions of friendship, a major component of personal letter writing, are a primary theme of 1 Thessalonians; they comprise fully half the letter. They are nevertheless directed in the official manner to the whole congregation, and this address is emphasized by the repeated apostrophes to 'adelphoi' — there are eleven of them. These expressions are more than social conventions; they form the basis for the messages. Paul has set forth a review of his ministry at Thessalonica; the review, in turn, sets the stage for his homilia. He must now, in the present situation, assume his teaching office by repeating or updating former instructions, or by offering new ones in response to Timothy's report.

The second portion of the letter conveys Paul's responses and instructions. It is replete with verbs meaning "to beseech" or "to exhort." These, according to Carl Bjerkelung, are most reminiscent of royal letters.[7] Yet Paul repeatedly relates the directives he makes in writing to his former oral word, an indication of his hesitancy to resort to writing (see below).

The ending of 1 Thessalonians is hardly a subscription; next to other Pauline letters it appears comparatively formless.[8] In it Paul restates his pastoral concerns and expresses tentative confidence in the letter's effectiveness in closing. There is a blessing (5:23-24), a request for prayer (v. 25), instruction to greet one another with the holy kiss (v. 26), a strongly adjured admonition that the letter be read to all members (v. 27), and, finally, a benediction (v. 28). There is no autographic subscription; in this letter Paul depends on the co-senders to confirm the letter-event (although it is possible that he wrote the final admoni-

---

own self'" (J. Gillman, "Paul's *EISODOS*" [67]). For expression of friendship in official letters see section on Philippians below.

7. Bjerkelund finds the occurrences of the *parakalô* periods gathered in chaps. 4-5. See his grouping of the occurrences and his discussion of their significance (Carl J. Bjerkelund, *Parakalô: Form, Funktion und Sinn der parakalô-Sätze in den paulinischen Briefen* [Oslo: Universitetsforlaget, 1967], 129-35). See his section, "Die Inschriften," 59-74; cf. Malherbe, *Paul and the Thessalonians* (above, note 2), 68-78.

8. Bahr writes, "1 Thessalonians gives no indication that it was written in two hands." He says that if he were to conjecture that the letter might have been composed by two hands, he would begin a second hand at 4:1 (Gordon J. Bahr, "The Subscriptions in the Pauline Letters," *JBL* 87 [1968]: 36). I see early elements of a subscription in 5:23-28 as listed in the text.

tion, "I adjure you by the Lord that this letter be read to all the brothers and sisters").[9]

Fairly early in his ministry Paul must have realized that he would be required to conduct a significant portion of his ministry from a distance, and that he must bridge the gap with letters as well as with emissaries. An emissary, after all, could convey back and forth a mutual exchange of messages, but only a written communication could really effectively convey a sense of his presence and authority (an end he highly desired — see 2:17-18). There is a hesitancy in 1 Thessalonians that suggests it was one of Paul's earliest attempts to adapt the official letter-form to his ministry. Paul is only beginning to discover the use and the force of the interdependence of oral and written messages in official communication.[10] Simply put, to write down that which he was accustomed to deliver orally, whether in person or by emissary, was an innovation that required a break with the oral milieu in which he was accustomed to preach and teach. Letter writing was the medium to aid in and effect this transition. At this early point in his epistolary ministry, perhaps encouraged by the co-senders, Paul makes bold to adopt the common means of communication, to reduce his oral word to written form, and to convey the sense of his personal presence. The challenge makes his consciousness of separation and desire to be present all the more pronounced.

It is in this instructional portion of the letter that Paul's initial reservations about writing become evident. His sensitivity is seen when he intersperses repetition of his previous oral instruction and doctrine with rhetorical or apologetic phrases. He writes:

> we beseech and exhort you in the Lord [now in writing] . . . as you
> learned from us [orally]. (4:1)
> For you know what instruction we gave you [orally] (4:2)
> . . . just as we have already told you beforehand and solemnly fore-
> warned you [orally and now in writing]. (4:6b)

9. Collins sees in the admonition to have the letter read before the congregation a mark of Paul's early use of letter writing. Raymond F. Collins, "'I Command That This Letter Be Read': Writing as a Manner of Speaking," in Karl P. Donfried and Johannes Beutler (eds.), *The Thessalonians Debate* (above, note 6), 328.

10. For the interdependence of letter and emissary see Chapter I, "The Logistics of Ancient Greek Letter Writing," 16.

regarding love of brothers no need to have anyone write to you.
(4:9)[11]

we exhort you [now] . . . as we charged you [formerly]. (4:10b-11)

we would not have you ignorant concerning those who are asleep.
(4:13)

regarding times and seasons you have no need to have anything
written to you. (5:1)

The phrase "you do not need" is a rhetorical device, but its repeated use also veils Paul's diffidence in writing, and his insistent notice that he is repeating (in writing) previous (oral) instructions allows him to secure the written word on the oral. He shows other evidence of uncertainty in writing. As noted above, the first person plurals emphasize the role of co-senders; but they also reveal a need on Paul's part to share not only the responsibility for the establishment and continued welfare of the congregation but also the responsibility for the subsequent visit and his present response. He assumes his individual responsibility in declaring his desire to visit, for his presence to be felt (2:17-18), and in the commissioning of Timothy (3:5). The introduction to the hortatory section disguises a mild apology for writing,

> Finally, brothers and sisters, we ask and urge you in the Lord Jesus that, as you learned from us how you ought to live and to please God (as, in fact, you are doing), you should do so more and more.

11. Collins interprets the preterition ("no need to write") as a rhetorical device used to emphasize a point. It may also mark a written form introducing a repetition of what had been originally spoken before the assembly. Thus in 4:9-12, Timothy has surely reported the continued mutual affection among the people. Paul only wants to show his appreciation for this report and now adds his ways of sustaining such a life. He says in recollection of his oral teaching, ". . . as we directed you" (4:11, fin.). In 5:1-11 Paul condenses instructions formerly given to the assembly in person but now in writing. Note ". . . you do not need to have anything written to you" (v. 1). This again seems to be in answer to Timothy's report as indicated by the closing phrase, ". . . as indeed you are doing" (v. 11). In 1:8 concerning the widespread reputation of the Thessalonians, Paul uses the verb "say." The reputation is well known ". . . so that we have no need to speak about it" (v. 8). Paul wants only to add his voice to the clamor of many others. Raymond F. Collins, "'I Command That This Letter Be Read': Writing as a Manner of Speaking," in Karl P. Donfried and Johannes Beutler (eds.), *The Thessalonians Debate* (above, note 6), 320-21. See how Paul extends this device in Phlm 8-9.

> For you know what instruction we gave you [orally] through the Lord Jesus. (1 Thess. 4:1-2, NRSV)

Joseph Plevnik writes, "In no other letter does the apostle make so many allusions to what the community has already learned from him. . . . His earlier instruction to the Thessalonians is still very fresh in his mind."[12] Notice that here Paul calls attention to the source of his word; he writes "in the Lord Jesus" just as he formerly instructed them "through the Lord Jesus" (4:1-2). And the order of the last events Paul declares to be "by the word of the Lord" (4:15).

B. 1 Corinthians

In 1 Corinthians, Paul shows a great deal more confidence in using the written word to carry out his ministry.[13] The spirit of pastoral warmth so prominent in 1 Thessalonians is now a secondary theme. To be sure, Paul casts himself as the Corinthians' nourishing parent (3:1-4) and father (4:14), and espouses love as the solution to problems within the church (13; 16:14, 20b, 24). But now he is in a different position. He is responding not to reports brought by his own emissary but to intelligence from representatives of the Corinthian church, delivered in the midst of strained relationships (1:10; 7:1). In the manner of an official who must respond to envoys from his jurisdiction, Paul responds with apostolic authority and with sure confidence in the medium he uses. He states his full identity: "Paul, called by the will of God to be an apostle of Jesus Christ . . ." and he names Sosthenes as his co-sender. Also in the manner of the official letter Paul writes from a more detached posi-

---

12. See Joseph Plevnik, "Pauline Presuppositions," in Collins (ed.), *Thessalonian Correspondence* (above, note 4), 53-54. Cf. Malherbe, *Paul and the Thessalonians* (above, note 2) 60. Donfried relates the repetition of "you know" and similar phrases to Paul's defense of his gospel (Karl P. Donfried [preceding note], 256-57). I see them as evidence of his being self-conscious in writing that which he is accustomed to give orally. See esp. 4:1, 2, 6, 10, 11.

13. I consider the letter a unit; so William F. Orr and James Arthur Walther, *I Corinthians: A New Translation*, Anchor Bible (Garden City, NY: Doubleday, 1976), 121-22; also Linda L. Belleville, "Continuity and Discontinuity: A Fresh Look at 1 Corinthians in the Light of First-Century Epistolary Forms and Conventions," *Evangelical Quarterly* 59 (1987): 15-37.

tion. Even the threat of a visit in person (4:17-21) is rhetorical, not betraying any genuine desire to be immediately present.[14]

Timothy is a deputized emissary (4:17; 16:10-11), and Paul writes from within a community to a community. He mentions the strong support he is receiving at his present locale (16:12, 19-20), and he reminds the people of the internal support that he enjoys at Corinth (16:15-18). Furthermore the relationship between Paul and the congregation is confirmed by the presence of Stephanas, Fortunatus, and Achaicus, who convey the good wishes of their home congregation to Paul and to the local community (16:17-18).[15] Whatever the intention of Timothy's trip (he will corroborate at least some of the instruction, 4:17), Paul is relying on the letter to deliver in written form and with authority his responses to the troubles at Corinth.

What experiences Paul had with written communication between the writing of 1 Thessalonians and 1 Corinthians cannot be known. This much is indicated: the oral and written reports from Corinth demand responses. And those responses must be made in writing, and they result in the longest letter written to a congregation founded by Paul. The range of topics addressed stands in contrast to the more limited subjects in 1 Thessalonians, and the seriatim treatment of the responses analyzed below suggests that Paul has realized his position as an intermediary and developed confidence in the medium and adaptability in using it.[16] It also argues for the unity of the letter.

14. The factions at Corinth have called forth a review and a defense of Paul's ministry in answer to opposition. He writes, "But some of you, thinking that I am not coming to you, have become arrogant. But I will come to you soon. What would you prefer? Am I to come to you with a stick, or with love in a spirit of gentleness?" (4:18-21). These verses are ironic. The rhetorical nature of the rhetorical questions is shown by their incompatibility with the two latter sections in the letter dealing with *parousia*. In chapter 5 Paul turns to his decision concerning the immoral man at Corinth. In it he clearly extends his presence and authority into the congregation by means of the letter. He certainly expected the letter to be equally effective in the problem of factions. Also the travel plans and reasons for visiting given at the end of the letter (16:1-9) make no mention of factions, the immoral man, nor any of the subjects treated in this letter. He has dismissed these matters. For the unity of 1 Cor see below.

15. For this writer's identification of Chloe's delegation with the delegation headed by Stephanas, see below.

16. For the contents see sections as divided for commentary by Roy A. Harrisville, *1 Corinthians*, Augsburg Commentary on the New Testament (Minneapolis: Augsburg,

1. 1 Corinthians and a Letter from Claudius to Alexandria

First Corinthians represents a fairly common type of letter in which the writer responds to requests and problems seriatim, using *peri de* to introduce the items. A secular representative of this type is a letter from the Emperor Claudius to the people of Alexandria.[17] Similarities in the form and the items treated offer some insights toward the interpretation of 1 Corinthians.

a. Recognition of Emissaries

The personal commendation and acknowledgment of the emissaries in each letter is a striking feature. Claudius names twelve envoys at the beginning of the letter; they have come to Claudius with a decree of honor and a list of requests. The emperor singles out three for special notice. He records the opposition of Dionysius to his dubbing the disturbance at Alexandria a war (ll. 73-76); and at the close he pays tribute to two others, Barbillus and Archibios (ll. 105-108). He says, "I bear witness to my friend, Barbillus, who has always had consideration for you before me and who, on this occasion, has fully advocated your case, as well as to my friend, Tiberius Claudius Archibios."

Paul does not generally name emissaries at the beginning of his letters. But in 1 Corinthians he recognizes the members of Chloe's delegation, albeit not by name. Perhaps naming them is unnecessary; certainly they are well known both to Paul and to the Corinthians. At the

---

1987); Jan Lambrecht, "A Structural Analysis of 1 Thessalonians 4-5," in Donfried and Beutler, *The Thessalonians Debate* (above, note 6), 163-78.

17. John L. White, *Light from Ancient Letters* (Philadelphia: Fortress, 1986), no. 88;* cf. Sherk, *Roman Documents from the Greek East* (Baltimore: Johns Hopkins Press, 1969), no. 26. For the *peri de* structure in a personal letter see no. 65 = *PYale* 42 in Chan-Hie Kim and John L. White, *Letters from the Papyri: A Study Collection,* Consultation on Ancient Epistolography, SBL Epistolography Seminar, 1974 (unpublished), hereafter = K & W; and in a personal letter between two officials, Nechthosiris to Leon, no. 28 in White, *Light.* The first portion of the latter letter contains the main items the chief of which is a request for Leon to see why a third party has not sent a cloak, tunic, and bread as requested. Thereafter the writer introduces two items each introduced by *peri de* and apparently in answer to a communication from Leon: "Concerning my affairs . . ." and "Concerning your brother. . . ."

close of the letter, then, he finds it worthwhile to name Stephanas, Fortunatas, and Achaicus (16:15-18). (It is possible that these three are in fact Chloe's delegation, but more on that later.) Stephanas, like Barbillus, is singled out for special commendation for being among the first converts at Corinth (v. 15). The apostle writes, "I rejoice at the coming of Stephanas and Fortunatus and Achaicus because they have made up for your absence; for they refreshed my spirit as well as yours. So give recognition to such persons" (vv. 17-18). In both letters, then, one may interpret the atypical personalizing of references to emissaries as commendation for the significant role they have played in presenting and helping to resolve the conflict at hand.

b. Transition

Claudius' transition to the body moves from a lengthy recording of mutual goodwill (ll. 20-27) to the direct statement, "Wherefore *(dioper)*, I willingly accept the honors . . ." (l. 28), and to the details of acceptance (ll. 29ff.).

Paul's transition is by suggestion. He reminds the Corinthians that they were called into fellowship *(koinōnia)* with Christ (1:9), and moves to an appeal for agreement and healing of divisions (i.e., for *koinōnia*, 1:10).

c. Major Topics

Claudius treats only one item in this section: the reception of honors. He responds to each honor offered by the decree after having heard the envoys at length but also after having had time to review the decree. Paul, in response to the oral reports, treats factions within the Corinthian church as the chief item. Neither Claudius nor Paul introduces these first items with *peri de.*

d. The Significance of the Absence of Peri De

The absence of *peri de* in the first item in each letter gives the item its significance. It is the basis for Claudius' generosity in the later decisions regarding matters that the Alexandrians have been anxious to receive (l. 52). For Paul it serves as the thematic topic for the whole letter;

factions underlie the various forms of wrongdoing.[18] That is, it was a major item in the written report from Chloe and also the major item in the oral discussion.

e. The Significance of Itemizing with Peri De

The writers' use of *peri de* in each letter indicates the consideration of specific written requests. In Claudius' letter, I interpret the *peri de* items as given in response to previous written requests. They are introduced with a general statement, "Concerning the requests which you have been anxious *(espoudakate)* to receive from me, I decide as follows," and were not part of the decree. The fact that the Alexandrians had been anxious (perfect tense) to hear from Claudius indicates that the matters had been put to him before. The interpretation, therefore, is that the envoys reminded Claudius of these requests, and he in turn (through the imperial secretaries) responded to them from previously written documents. In his letters, Paul clearly marks the transition between responses to oral and written reports (1:11; 7:1). The tag *peri de* in both letters introduces itemized responses to reports from written documents.

f. Interpretation of the Itemization

The first item in each letter (for Claudius, honors; for Paul, factions) should be considered the chief item. Its immediate consideration, the length of its treatment, and its recurrence in subsequent items all attest to its relative sgnificance. The absence of *peri de,* too, in this first item indicates that the writers are treating items chiefly, if not wholly, recalled from oral presentations, the result of dialogue with Alexandrian envoys and Chloe's emissaries. Thus the decree on Claudius' behalf would include reference to the Alexandrians' goodwill. In response Claudius adds his own and includes the contributions of Germanicus (l. 27). These items would first arise in the oral exchanges.

In like manner for Paul's letter the omission of *peri de* sets the item

---

18. For the thematic topic, see Linda L. Belleville, *Reflections of Glory: Paul's Polemical Use of the Moses-Doxa Tradition in 2 Corinthians 3:1-18,* JSNT Sup. 52 (Sheffield: JSOT Press, 1991), 120-35.

apart from the following series and gives it thematic prominence. Paul marks this prominence by beginning with a *parakalō* sentence, "Now I appeal to you . . ." (1:10).[19] This emphasis is also shown by the well-marked transition phrase by which Paul turns his attention away from the oral discussion to the items in the letter from Corinth (7:1). In this interpretation the oral presentation also included sexual immorality (5:1-13) and lawsuits (6:1-11); for they also are not introduced by *peri de*. It is indicated, therefore, that they were offered by the emissaries as the significant causes of divisions. Paul returns to these subjects and gives them first consideration in his subsequent discussion. Very likely the report concerning the immoral man at Corinth was used by Chloe's people to offer a specific example of the problem with marriage at Corinth. So Paul treats marriage in full (chap. 7), and lawsuits are included with other wrongdoings (6:9-11). Thereupon Paul adds an excursus on the rights of an apostle and the conduct of his ministry — perhaps called forth in defense of his single lifestyle (chap. 9).

g. Specific Responses

In both letters the writers take the opportunity to make comments on the specific response, to express personal reactions, and to offer themselves as models.

For example, in considering the "Jewish Question" Claudius says,

> Simply stated, if you do not lay to rest this destructive and obstinate hostility against one another, I shall be forced to show what a benevolent ruler can become when turned to [inflict] a justified wrath. (ll. 79-81)[20]

---

19. For the significance of the verb, see Bjerkelund, *Parakalô* (above, note 7), 141. Cf. Dahl, *Studies* (below, note 24), 46. See above section, "1 Thessalonians."

20. Claudius asserts himself with expressions of his feelings which are in rather self-serving terms. He says. "Wherefore, I willingly *(hedeōs)* accept the honors given by you to me, even though I have no taste for such things" (line 28; note that, nevertheless, he gives thorough consideration to each item). ". . . the construction of temples, I deprecate, not wishing to be offensive to my contemporaries and because I consider temples and the like to be set apart in all ages for the gods alone" (ll. 48-51; note "deified Augustus" and reference to his temple, ll. 60-62; hint at the possibility of a deified Claudius).

In response to the oral reports, Paul defines true apostleship (3:1–4:5) and presents himself as example. Thus,

> When I came to you, brothers and sisters, I did not come proclaiming the mystery of God in lofty words of wisdom. For I decided to know nothing among you but Jesus Christ and him crucified. (2:1-2)[21]

h. Threats and Warnings

Another similarity in the two letters under consideration involves their strongly worded threats and warnings. Twice Claudius expresses his reactions to the disturbance in Alexandria, the first already quoted above:

> Simply stated, if you do not lay to rest this destructive and obstinate hostility against one another, I shall be forced to show what a benevolent ruler can become when turned to [inflict] a justified wrath. (ll. 79-81)

> Otherwise, I will take vengeance against them in every respect, just as though they were a widespread plague infecting the whole inhabited world. (ll. 98-100)

And Paul writes:

> But I will come to you soon, if the Lord wills, and will find out not the talk of these arrogant people but their power. (4:19)

> For all who eat and drink without discerning the body, eat and drink judgment against themselves. (11:29)

> Let anyone be accursed who has no love for the Lord. (16:22)

Intense and long consultations on the troubles at both home bases drew from the writers' strong feelings — perhaps reflecting the mood and spirit of the conference.

---

21. See also, "I planted, Apollos watered, but God gave the growth" (3:6); "I appeal to you then be imitators of me" (4:16, cf. 10:31–11:1); "I wish that all were as I myself am" (7:8, regarding celibacy).

i. Promise

Claudius adds a conventional promise after the last threat:

> [But] if you both [Alexandrians and Jews] forsake such things and
> are willing to live with gentleness and kindness toward one an-
> other, I, for my part, will have the greatest consideration for the
> city, just as one which has a long-standing familiar status with us.
> (ll. 101-104)

Paul's promises are indirect. At the very beginning, in the thanksgiving and therefore rather conventionally, he reminds the Corinthians
of the effects of Christ's grace upon them,

> He [Christ] will strengthen you to the end, so that you may be
> blameless on the day of our Lord Jesus Christ. (1:8)

And at the end, after the excursus on the resurrection, Paul gives an admonition that implies a promise,

> Therefore, my beloved, be steadfast, immovable, always excelling
> in the work of the Lord, because you know that in the Lord your
> labor is not in vain. (15:58)

j. Pauline Excursuses

The settings, the writers' official positions, their purposes in writing,
and the final dispositions of the communications make for differences
in length and content. Claudius writes in anticipation that his document will be permanently recorded on stone. Brevity, therefore, is of
some importance, though he does write at some length when responding to each proffered honor, and he writes in detail concerning the Jewish question. Paul, on the other hand, writes on papyrus or parchment
for immediate use and is free to include extra sheets for excursuses. For
example, as a closure to the two items from the oral presentation on
sexual immorality and lawsuits, Paul adds a section on the sins of the
flesh and on the body as the temple of the Holy Spirit (6:9-20). And excurses are inserted after the consideration of the first items in the letter
from Corinth (7 and 8): Apostolic rights, Christian freedom, and the

limits imposed by the rights of others (9:1–11:1), and behavior in and conduct of worship (11:2-34).

Paul returns to the items introduced by *peri de,* "Now concerning spiritual gifts . . ." (12:1–14:25), and more excursuses follow: further instructions regarding worship (14:26-40); the resurrection (15:1-58), and, finally, the last *peri de* item, "Now concerning the collection for the saints . . ." (16:1-4).

Thus the organization of 1 Corinthians is essentially this: first, the responses to the orally presented items; and second, the responses to the written communication.[22] Within this simple, officially patterned order Paul inserts for various reasons and from various sources matters he thinks to be helpful in the Corinthian situation. He draws on the discussion with Chloe's emissaries, from his previous relations with the people, from his general ministerial experiences, especially those pertinent ones in which he can offer himself as model.

k. Conclusion

In view of the official letter-form as determined by comparison with Claudius' letter, it is the conclusion of this writer that Paul's letter is a single document. Seriatim letters covering numerous items from several sources do not necessarily yield to logical organization of the elements.[23] It also seems that Paul is responding to a single delegation

---

22. Mitchell states emphatically Paul's freedom in responding to Corinth, "In 1 Corinthians we see a Paul himself in control of his material and his medium, not a Paul enslaved to the order or logic of his communiques from Corinth" (Margaret M. Mitchell, *Paul and the Rhetoric of Reconciliation: An Exegetical Investigation of the Language and Composition of 1 Corinthians,* HUT 28 [Tübingen: Mohr/Siebeck, 1991; Louisville: Westminster/ John Knox, 1992], 297). Mitchell summarizes her work, "This investigation, through an exegetical study of the language and composition of 1 Corinthians, with particular utilization of the method of historical rhetorical criticism, has argued that 1 Corinthians is a unified deliberative letter which throughout urges unity on the divided Corinthian church" (296).

23. In regard to Paul's order of responses, Baird observes, "Paul treats the conflict according to the problems that have been raised by his sources of information. Thus particular problems, not factions, order the argument, so that the factions must be detected in relation to the problems" (William Baird, "'One Against the Other': Intra-Church Conflict in 1 Corinthians," in Robert T. Fortna and Beverly R. Gaventa [eds.], *The Conversation Continues: Studies in Paul and John in Honor of J. Louis Martyn* [Nashville:

from Corinth; the single document responds to a single source.[24] The reasons for identifying but one delegation are,

1. Among official letters there is no example of the dispatch of two delegations from the same base, on the same mission at approximately the same time, one with oral messages and one with written messages.[25]
2. An emissary carried the written document and spoke to it. This double assignment was the common function of emissaries. According to protocol, the delegates first delivered the oral mes-

---

Abingdon, 1990], 116-36; the quotation is from p. 131). See Baird's review of the history of research on factions at Corinth (116-18). Demosthenes responds to a letter from Philip item by item, *Or.* 7 (*On Halonnesus*). Cf. 1 Cor 7:1, 25; 8:1; 12:1; 16:1, 12; 1 Thess 4:9, 13; 5:14. An official responds to matters presented to him, usually to a single or limited number of requests, but in the case of Paul's and Claudius' letters the requests and problems are multiple, and they reply to them accordingly. Mitchell finds a consistent rhetorical theme in 1 Cor (Margaret M. Mitchell, *Paul and the Rhetoric of Reconciliation* [preceding note]. See esp. Chap. IV, "Compositional Analysis: 1 Corinthians as a Unified Deliberative Letter Urging Concord," 184-295).

24. Dahl supports two separate emissaries from Corinth. He says, "In all probability, the Corinthians had commissioned these delegates [the three named] to bring a letter from the congregation to Paul, asking for his opinion on a number of questions. In this letter it was stated that the Corinthians remembered Paul in everything and maintained the traditions he had delivered to them [1 Cor 11:2]. Thus the official attitude of the congregation seems to have been one of loyalty to the apostle. Yet Chloe's people could orally report that there was strife in Corinth and that there was some opposition to Paul. The tension between the written document and the oral report requires some explanation" (Nils Alstrup Dahl, *Studies in Paul* [Minneapolis: Augsburg, 1977], 50; see his explanation 52-55). The tension and hostility are in the situation at Corinth. These matters were reported in the oral meeting; they were not subjects of the letter. The tension in 1 Cor is similar to the tension in Claudius' letter. The decree that the envoys brought to Claudius was irenic; their oral report on the Jewish question revealed the hostility at Alexandria.

25. Note that Claudius is responding to one Greek emissary bringing the decree and speaking at length. See White's (and Tcherikover's) suggestion that the difficult lines 90-91 refer to two previous emissaries from the Jews to Claudius with ". . . a considerable difference of opinion between the two . . ." (John L. White, *Light* [above, note 17], 132). This could be a similar occasion to the Corinthian event, but the interpretation between the two sets of envoys, the occasions for presentation, the means of communication (oral, written, or both), and the reason for the missions are entirely unknown. A different situation exists in Welles, *Royal Cor.*, no. 7: two sets of envoys, one from Samos and one from Priene, were sent to Lysimachus because of a boundary dispute between the two cities.

sages, speaking both about the document and on other subjects as well. They then delivered the written document for later, fuller, consideration and response by the recipient. Emissaries to and from Paul played this dual role.[26]

3. The absence of *peri de* marks the responses to oral presentations; its presence, the responses to written items. As with Claudius, there is no reason to doubt that both types of messages were delivered to Paul on the same occasion.

4. The influence of oral presentations and resulting discussion may resurface and be reflected in a written response to the emissary's home base. Thus Paul has repetitions and extensions of concern about sex and marriage relations.

It is, therefore, the interpretation of this writer that the reports from Corinth were brought by a single delegation. Chloe's delegation is mentioned at the beginning of the letter, though, as is typical of him, Paul does not name the individuals who comprise it. At the end three people are named who were also members of Chloe's deputation. It is a customary practice in official letters to refer to an emissary in closing, a custom which Paul here observes.[27]

Chloe and the three named are strong supporters of Paul. Chloe was a person of influence, probably the chief representative, if not the head, of the party claiming allegiance to Paul (1:12; 3:4, 22). As a woman, she would not have accompanied the emissaries. But the emissaries are "of" or "from" her, though she is not named at the close of the letter along with those who conducted the mission. Someone has acted with organizational abilities and with concern that transcends the factions, whatever his or her personal allegiance may have been. Chloe seems to have been such a person. She was certainly aided and supported by the three people recognized at the end. It is also possible that the political position apparent throughout Paul's letter originated with Chloe. Paul refers to the letter from Corinth as containing "the matters about which you [pl.] wrote . . ." (7:1). The plural refers to the whole Corinthian congregation to which Paul's responses were made. Perhaps this

---

26. For the role of envoys, see Chap. I, "Logistics," 11-16.

27. Paul does not elsewhere name emissaries sent to him — even in Galatians. See below.

avoidance of specifying individuals or factions was Chloe's position. The one who drafted the letter from Corinth (again, Chloe?) saw to it that it was written in the name of all the people, and Paul agreed with this position and responded in kind. He does not address any faction openly or by the name of its patron.

Regarding the letter-body, in a seriatim letter — a letter made up of a series of responses to problems and questions — the body as a whole does not readily allow the twofold division of background and message. However, it is noteworthy that some of the units in the series of responses display this typical official letter-form and are designated "sub-letter forms." For example (White, *Light*, no. 88*):

Claudius,
  Background, a general reference to former requests,
    — "Concerning the requests which you have been anxious to receive from me," (l. 52)
  Decision announced,
    — "I decide as follows," (l. 53a)
  Specific decisions (ll. 53b-65):
    — citizenship of the *epheboi* (ll. 53b-57a)
    — confirmation of matter granted in former times (ll. 57b-59)
    — choosing by lot of the temple overseers (ll. 60-62a)
    — approval of triennial terms for municipal magistrates (ll. 62b-66a).

And,
  Background, announcement of subject,
    — "As to who should be held responsible for the disorder and sedition against the Jews . . . ," (l. 73) (gen. without *peri de*)
  Personal ground for decision,
    — "I have not desired to make a detailed examination . . . but I have stored up within me an immutable hostility against those who renewed the conflict." (ll. 78-84) (Note that the opposition of Dionysius, one of the envoys, to Claudius' position is recorded.)
  Decision
    — a. Threat,
        "Simply stated, if you do not lay to rest this destructive and ob-

*stinate hostility against one another, I shall be forced to show
what a benevolent ruler can become when turned to [inflict] a
justified wrath."* (ll. 79-81)
— b. Admonition to the Alexandrians (ll. 82-88a)
— c. Orders to the Jews *(keleuō)* (ll. 88b-98a)
— d. Additional threat (ll. 89b-100)
> *"[If the Jews admit refugees] I will be forced to conceive an even
> more serious suspicion. Otherwise I will take vengeance against
> them in every respect. . . ."*
— e. Promise (ll. 101-4)

This final unit is the second major item. It too is lengthy and, unless
peri de was mistakenly omitted, it begins only with the genitive, *tēs de
pros Iudaious taraxēs . . .* (l. 73).[28]

In like manner, Paul uses the body sub-form to make the difficult
response in the case of the immoral person at Corinth. The elements in
the two units are discernible: (1) background which consists of "the
other side of the dialogue"; (2) decision and basis for decision; (3) admonition; (4) closing. Thus,

Chapter 5:1-8,
1. background: reiteration of the report, "It is actually reported
    that there is sexual immorality among you. . . ." (vv. 1-2)
2. decision and basis for decision: ". . . you are to hand this man
    over to Satan so that his spirit may be saved. . . ." (vv. 3-5)
3. admonition: "Clean out the old yeast. . . ." (vv. 6-7)
4. closing: "Therefore, let us celebrate the festival. . . ." (v. 8)

28. In Claudius' letter, after acknowledging the ambassadors, Claudius reports on
their delivery of the decree, their speaking at length, and their expression of the Alexandrians' goodwill. Then the unit deals at length with honors the Alexandrians wish to
bestow on him. The sub-form introduces the acceptance of honors: Background as
ground for decision, "For it [Alexandrian goodwill] arises because you are reverent by nature regarding the Augusti . . . and zealously reciprocated by my own family . . ." (ll. 23-27);
Decision, "Wherefore [*dioper*], I willing accept the honors given by you to me, even
though I have no taste for such things" (ll. 28-29). See also, Background, announcement
of the subject, "Regarding the senate, what indeed your custom was under the kings, I
have no means of saying. . . ." (ll. 66b-69a). Ground for delayed decision, "Because this is
now a new matter . . . and it is uncertain whether it will be advantageous . . ." (ll. 86b-70a).
Tentative decision, "I wrote to Aemilius Rectus to examine the matter . . ." (ll. 70b-72).

Chapter 5:9-13,

1a. background past: reference to previous, misinterpreted letter, "I wrote to you in my letter not to associate with sexually immoral persons. . . ." (vv. 9-10)

1b. background present: "But now I am writing to you not to associate with anyone . . . who is sexually immoral. . . ." (v. 11)

2. basis for decision, the role of judgment: "God will judge those outside." (vv. 12-13a)

3. decision: "Drive out the wicked person from among you. (v. 13b)

These short, terse responses from Paul to the reports on sexual immorality, their central place in the responses, and the use of the subform that is similar to the autographic subscriptions, suggest that Paul penned these verses as he did the subscriptions. This subject was reported orally (chap. 5), and in the first response to the letter from Corinth (chap. 7) he added instructions for marriage relations. This subject was a chief concern and Paul may well have written the directives with his own hand.

C. 2 Corinthians

The textual problems in the present 2 Corinthians, especially the marked divisions and transitions, make formal analysis difficult. We can say only a few things with certainty, and these have to do primarily with the salutation on the letter.

The first portion of the present 2 Corinthians (chapters 1-7) is a paean of joy and consolation over Paul's reconciliation with the Corinthians. The movement from deep anxiety through autobiographic apology through the comfort of reconciliation to rejoicing is personal and pastoral.[29] Interestingly, even in this more personal letter Paul

---

29. Linda L. Belleville, *Reflections of Glory* (above, note 18), 121. Belleville reviews the many suggestions concerning the type of letter represented by chapters 1-7. She writes, "The major difficulty with all the preceding suggestions is that elements of each letter type can be found in 2 Corinthians 1-7. Indeed, the models for each type of letter suggested can be found in the epistolary handbooks of the period. Yet none of these types accounts for the epistolary movement from disclosure (1.8ff.) to request (6.1ff.) found in 2 Corinthians 1-7." Belleville calls these chapters, "an official letter of apologetic self-

adopts elements of the official setting. The salutation follows a full complement of units: sender identity, co-sender, and multiple recipients. The recipients are "all the saints in Achaia." This salutation will be compared below with that of 1 Corinthians; a similar inclusive address is suggested by Welles on one of the royal letters.

This intimate address is followed by a section (chapters 8 and 9) that is much more official in tone. These two chapters form a copy or paraphrase of the letter (or letters) authorizing the collection of the Famine Relief Fund; they are a letter of commendation and authorization of the commission. Titus alone is named (8:6, 16, 23); he seems to be designated leader of the commission. If the section is a conflation of separate letters (chapters 8 and 9 respectively) the forms would have been by protocol official; if they are conflated, the editor continued to show that form. Thus, background, 8:1-6; request, 8:7-8; basis and explanation (the example of Christ), 8:9-15; the request actualized (by introduction and authorization of the commission), 8:16–9:5; admonition, 9:6-7; conclusion (the promise, 11a), 9:8-12; closing and benediction, 9:13-15.[30]

The official tenor of a letter is set by its salutation. The multiple address on 1 and 2 Corinthians is of special significance and is comparable to a letter addressed to the Guild of Dionysiac Artists (see below). The multiple address on 2 Corinthians reads,

> To the church of God being in Corinth along with all the saints in the whole of Achaia. (1:1, translation by the author)

---

commendation" *(ibid.,* 125-30). Crafton interprets 2 Cor as the conflation of portions of three letters in each of which Paul presents himself as an agent of three different manners (Jeffrey A. Crafton, *The Agency of the Apostle. A Dramatistic Analysis of Paul's Responses to Conflict in 2 Corinthians,* JSNT Sup 51 [1991]).

30. The editor may have inserted these chapters here to continue the general theme of commendation and recommendation throughout chapters 1-7 by recording the role of Titus on the commission to follow his high commendation in 6:5-13. Furnish sees the reference to Titus as showing that chaps. 8-9 were part of one letter with the preceding chapters, and in themselves formed one unit (Furnish, *II Cor.* [below, note 32], 35-44). I see the references to Titus as an editor's key for joining letter fragments. I have found no example of a letter of recommendation included in or attached to another letter. Letters of recommendation are independent documents in themselves. For the literature on 2 Cor 8-9 see Chap. I, "Logistics," note 47.

This is similar to that on 1 Corinthians,

> To the assembly of God being in Corinth sanctified in Christ Je-
> sus, called saints, along with all [saints] who call upon the name
> of our Lord Jesus Christ in every place. (i.e., their Lord and ours;
> 1 Cor 1:1, translation by the author)

By these headings Paul identifies himself with the larger jurisdiction
and with the major city of the region. Salutations such as these are
comparable to those of intermediate officials, who generally make reference to the larger constituency.[31]

This understanding of the salutations to the Corinthians supports
the interpretation of Furnish and Barrett and is further supported by
Welles, no. 53. Furnish writes,

> The form of the address implies that some kind of regularized
> contact was maintained between the Corinthian congregation
> and Christians in the outlying communities, and that Paul re-
> garded his letter as having some, if only secondary, meaning for
> them as well.[32]

---

31. For example, "King Attalus to the council and people of Cyzicus, greeting"
(Welles, *Royal Cor.*, 66). Such salutations are further extended and the recipients are
more specifically identified in letters from commanders to their armies. For example,
"King Antiochus to generals, cavalry and infantry officers, soldiers, and the rest [*tois
allois*], greeting" (Welles, no. 39). Welles notes, "This, except for *tois allois*, is an ordinary
heading of a general order to the army" *(Royal Cor.,* 170). Also, "King Ptolemy Philopator
to the generals and soldiers in Egypt and every place *(kata topon)*, greeting and good
health" (3 Macc 3:12; cf. 7:1; 1 Macc 14:20b).

32. Victor Paul Furnish, *II Corinthians,* The Anchor Bible (Garden City, NY: Doubleday, 1984), 106. See also Richard B. Hays, *First Corinthians* (Louisville: John Knox, 1997),
16-17. Hays speaks of a "network of communities of faith." It may also be noted that
Hauck suggests that the address on 2 Corinthians is the device of an editor who collected Paul's letters at Corinth and by this address directed them to all the Pauline
churches (Friedrich Hauck, *Die Entstehung des Neuen Testaments* [Gütersloh, 1949], 244-
45). Lietzmann and Kümmel suggest that the extended greeting is patterned on the Jewish liturgy (Hans Lietzmann, Werner Georg Kümmel, *An die Korinther I. II.* Commentary
on 1 Cor 1:1) [Tübingen: Mohr/Siebeck, 1949]). See Franz Schnider and Werner Stenger,
Studien (above, note 4), 22-23. Skeats considers the MS evidence (P[46]) concerning Paul's
inclusion of bishops and deacons as being inconclusive (T. C. Skeat, "Did Paul Write to
'Bishops and Deacons' at Philippi? A Note on Philippians 1:1," *NovT* 37 [1995]: 12-13). I ar-

Likewise Barrett:

> Probably all these persons [the saints throughout Achaia] would
> have an opportunity of learning the content of the letter; accord-
> ing to Hering we must think of a circular letter, but it is better to
> recall that Corinth was the capital, and that a letter sent to the
> church there would be likely in due course to find its way to outly-
> ing places where there were Christians.[33]

1. 2 Corinthians and a Letter to the Guild of Dionysiac Artists

The text of this letter to the Guild is too fragmentary to include any
part of it in the Appendix. As Welles has reconstructed it, however, it is
a fascinating parallel to 2 Corinthians — an open letter to the guilds in
various places. It supports the interpretation of the first portion of
Paul's letter as an open letter addressed to the people in Corinth and to
those scattered in Achaia. According to Welles, "the persons addressed
in the letter were in close relation to the city of Teos while being clearly
separated from it" (*Royal Correspondence*, p. 231).

The letter deals with disputed issues and complaints brought by envoys from the several locales. The response was inscribed and set up in
Teos. Whatever the wording of the original address, it most likely was a
general address to the members of the Guild and not to individuals or
even to the towns. That is, the letter was addressed to scattered members of the Guild who still held Teos as the controlling center of their
activities.

Second Corinthians reflects a similar setting. As already noted, Corinth was the hub for the ministry throughout Achaia. At any given time
in its assembly visitors and travelers were likely present. From the letter
to Teos it is possible to infer that Christians scattered in the region

---

gue that the similarity with official salutations explains Paul's extended address. For
the central location of Corinth see Chap. I, "Logistics," note 52.

33. C. K. Barrett, *A Commentary on the Second Epistle to the Corinthians* (New York:
Harper and Row, 1973), 55. Note that in addition to the church at Corinth Paul mentions
a church at Cenchreae (Rom 16:1). See Branick's discussion of Phoebe's work at
Cenchreae (Vincent P. Branick, *The House Church in the Writings of Paul* [Wilmington: Glazier, 1989], 65-66).

looked to Corinth as the center of their worship and instruction. By some means, Paul's communications would reach them.

D. Philippians

Philippians proves what 2 Corinthians only hints at: that Paul appropriates the forms and settings of the official letter regardless of the cause or intent of his communication. The major objective of this letter is to express friendship to the assembly. A letter from Antiochus to Erythrae shows that other official letter writers also sometimes include expressions of closeness. Although there are wide differences, as we shall see below, the similarity of items encourages a comparison and demonstrates again Paul's sense of being an apostolic intermediary in all relationships with the assemblies.

Another indirectly related matter pertains to this letter. Studies on friendship and related subjects by members of the Society of Biblical Literature's Hellenistic Moral Philosophy and Early Christianity Group devote special attention to Philippians. These analyses are based on personal letter writing and commentaries on personal letters. But evidence suggests that Philippians, like Paul's other letters, is officially apostolic, and not personal.

I will begin by briefly offering a summary of the basic official letter-forms and setting as they are evident in Philippians: Paul is in prison, perhaps on death row, and it seems that in some way the choice between life and death is his (1:22b; 2:17). He writes, nevertheless, out of a community of supporters: Timothy (1:1; 2:19-24), Epaphroditus (2:25-30), unnamed other brothers and sisters, and the saints of Caesar's household (4:21). Timothy is co-sender. Paul writes to a community: "To all the saints in Christ Jesus who are at Philippi, with the bishops and deacons," and the multiple address assures a public reading.

1. Philippians and a Letter from Antiochus to Erythrae

The expressions of friendship in Philippians are made especially noticeable through parallel expressions in a letter from Antiochus to Erythrae (Welles, no. 15*). The similar items in each letter include a rec-

ognition of ambassadors, the review of mutual goodwill, the acknowledgment of gifts, admonitions and blessings, and the strong but re-
served reliance on authority for decisions. Antiochus' letter grants a
request from the people of Erythrae, Paul responds to a report from
the people of Philippi.[34]

There are, to be sure, differences. The one letter is politically motivated; the other pastorally motivated. That difference in motivation in
each letter determines the tenor of the language. For Antiochus goodwill *(eunoia)* is secondary, intended for clothing an authoritative decree. For Paul authority is secondary, even incidental, to the expression
of affection *(agape)*, the major purpose of his writing. One letter is comparatively short, delivering two messages, prepared by a royal chancery
with conventional wording. The other is much longer, containing a collection of messages in extemporary expression, likely prepared with the
help of an ad hoc secretariat. Nevertheless, the congruencies and similarities make it possible to see Philippians in a context similar to that
of a secular letter of this type.

In both letters the ambassadors are highly commended. The three
from Antiochus are named at the beginning when they present the decree honoring the king, the wreath, and the gift of gold (line 2). They
are named again in the second part of the letter when they speak in
their own words on behalf of the mission and are accredited with its

---

34. I interpret Philippians as a single document. For evidence that the letter is
composite see Jürgen Becker, *Paul: Apostle to the Gentiles,* 307-15; Becker finds evidence
of two letters and reconstructs their original order. For the single letter hypothesis see
Stanley K. Stowers, "Friends and Enemies in the Politics of Heaven: Reading Theology
in Philippians," in Jouette M. Bassler (ed.), *Pauline Theology Vol. I: Thessalonians,
Philippians, Galatians, Philemon,* 105-21; see 114-17. Stowers sees in this "hortatory" letter
a pattern based on the behavior of friends and enemies. For the single letter hypothesis see also John Koenig's commentaries on Philippians and Philemon (Augsburg
Commentary on the New Testament [Minneapolis: Augsburg, 1985], 125-28). Reed contributes to the unity of Phil by his study of the hesitation formula of 3:1 (Jeffrey T.
Reed, "Philippians 3:1 and the Epistolary Hesitation Formulas: The Literary Integrity
of Philippians Again," *JBL* 115 [1990]: 63-90). The nature and accidents of Pauline letter
writing may account for the seeming disunity of this letter. He responds to numerous
messages from a congregation after a period of consultation with Timothy and
Epaphroditus. He writes or dictates extemporaneously with little opportunity for revision. Epaphroditus, as returning emissary, is free to add to and interpret the items of
the letter.

success (line 21). At the end they are again praised and charged to report to Erythrae:

> [More about these matters and] the other questions which we discussed [will be reported to you by your] envoys, whom [we praise for their conduct] and in general and especially for the concern they have shown [for the interests of your people]. Farewell.

Paul likewise recognizes and highly commends his emissaries, Timothy and Epaphroditus. Timothy is named as co-sender. He is identified as servant of Christ Jesus, and he receives a full recommendation when he is authorized as Paul's ambassador to Philippi (2:19-23). He is to make a round trip to Philippi, as Paul says, "so that I may be cheered by news of you" (2:19). And Paul expresses double delight in having had the services of Epaphroditus in both directions of his journey. Paul recognizes him as the Philippians' *apostolos* and *leitourgos,* but he also claims, commends, and sends him to Philippi as his "brother and fellow worker and fellow soldier" (2:25-30). He is named twice, at the beginning of the section introducing the specific messages (2:25; [3:2–4:7]); and in the acknowledgment of the gifts (4:18). It is implied that he will report on his stay with Paul and Paul's condition (2:28-29).

Each writer reviews the goodwill between himself and the people, and each notes that those feelings are rooted in the past and continue into the present: Antiochus and the council and people of Erythrae (lines 6-12; 15-21); Paul and all the saints in Philippi, the bishops and deacons (i.e., the "council" and people of Philippi, 1:3-11).

Both acknowledge gifts received from their correspondents: Antiochus, a decree of honor, a crowning wreath, and *xenia,* a friendship gift of gold (lines 3-5; 13-14); Paul, *doma,* an undesignated gift which likely included some money (4:17-18).

Both appeal for remembrance and steadfastness in their relationships. Antiochus: "We summon [*papakaloumen*] you also, remembering that [we have always] tried earnestly [to see to it] that you will remember suitably those [by whom] you have been benefitted" (lines 30-34). And Paul: "Keep on doing the things that you have learned and received and heard and seen in me, and the God of peace will be with you" (4:9).

And both promise reciprocal blessings: Antiochus, "[We grant your requests.] "You shall have also [. . . and] any other benefit which we think of or [you ask for]" (lines 28-30); and Paul, "And my God will fully satisfy every need of yours according to his riches in glory in Christ Jesus" (4:19; see also 4:9 above).

Both writers draw on their authority. For issuing a decree Antiochus will not be doubted or questioned; his position of power is expressed in generous but politically secure terms. Paul also must exercise his authority. Two problems at Philippi demand his immediate decisions — the contention concerning circumcision and the quarrel between Euodia and Syntyche (3:2-4:7).[35] He expects compliance with his instructions on the part of the Philippians (1:27-30).

2. Expressions of Friendship in Philippians

a. The Studies by the SBL Group on Hellenistic Moral Philosophy and Early Christianity

In spite of the differences between expressions of political goodwill and those of apostolic affection, Paul's letter still bears in its form the marks of his sense of writing as one who holds an official position. What is the source of Paul's expressions of friendship in Philippians? Clearly they originate in those relationships which are established and maintained with various degrees of intimacy and which lie deep in the patterns and needs of human society. The studies by the SBL Hellenistic Moral Philosophy and Early Christianity Group on friendship, both biblical and extra-biblical, offer valuable insights into the ways in which such feelings were expressed in the letters of the ancient world. The broad scope of these works describes the context of friendship as practiced in Paul's day.[36]

---

35. Concerning Paul's apostolic authority see Mitchell and his reference to Marshall who believes his study of friendship and enmity in the Corinthian correspondence leads to a more accurate picture of the struggle between Paul and his rivals (Alan C. Mitchell, S.J., "'Greet the Friends by Name': New Testament Evidence for the Greco-Roman *Topos* on Friendship," in John T. Fitzgerald [ed.], *Greco-Roman Perspectives on Friendship* [Atlanta: Scholars Press, 1996], 225-62. The quotation is from pp. 230-31 and the reference is to P. Marshall, *Enmity in Corinth* [1987]).

36. John T. Fitzgerald (ed.), *Friendship, Flattery, and Frankness of Speech: Studies on*

It should be stated that these studies on friendship are perforce largely based on personal letters and the ancient commentators and essayists who treat this type of letter; there is no equivalent handbook and little ancient discussion of official letter writing. But as I argued in Chapter II, "The Official Letter-Form and the Pauline Letters," the letters of the royal secretaries served as models for official letter writing — in effect, a handbook. Their letters and those of later writers who copy the royal models are, therefore, the proper source for determining the terminology. Still there are a number of insights that can be gained from the writings of the Group.

On the basis of his wider studies on moral philosophical thought and its reflection in Paul's writings, Abraham Malherbe selects a number of expressions of friendship and shows their evidences in Paul. For example, he treats a central problem current in the more technical language of the first century BCE — that is, how can the highly desired virtue of self-sufficiency be reconciled with the giving and receiving of benefits between friends?[37] He finds the answer in Cicero's *De Amicitia*. Cicero writes, ". . . to the extent that a man relies upon himself, to that degree he is most conspicuous in picking out and cherishing friendships" (*Amic.* 30). A friend seeks out friends for their good character and especially their virtue, characteristics which match and supplement one's own.

Malherbe reviews the verses in Philippians (4:10-20) which contain Paul's affirmation of his own self-sufficiency and says that God will also supply the Philippians' every need. He notes Paul's immersion in the current language and thought, but he also notes that he uses them for his purposes. He says, "Indeed, what Paul had already received was a

---

Friendship in the New Testament World (Leiden: E. J. Brill, 1996). In addition to the studies by the Group, Betz analyzes Gal 4:10-20 identifying Paul's dependence on friendship *topos*. His concern is with the elements of true friendship (Hans Dieter Betz, *Galatians: A Commentary on Paul's Letter to the Churches in Galatia* [Philadelphia: Fortress, 1979], 220-37). See Mitchell's summary of Betz' analysis and his identifying of the elements with commentary (Alan C. Mitchell, "'Greet the Friends by Name'" [above, note 35], 225-62).

37. Abraham J. Malherbe, "Paul's Self-Sufficiency (Philippians 4:11)," in Fitzgerald (ed.), *Friendship* (above, note 36), 125-39. Quotation from p. 135. See Berry's summary of the teaching of the philosophers concerning self-sufficiency (112-14) and his commentary on the various interpretations of Paul's self-sufficiency (115-23) (Ken L. Berry, "The Function of Friendship Language in Philippians 4:10-20," in Fitzgerald [ed.], *Friendship*, 107-24).

sacrificial gift acceptable to God (vs. 18). As he does elsewhere, then, Paul uses the moral philosophical language of his day, but places it within a larger framework quite foreign to the philosophical tradition he uses."[38]

John Fitzgerald collects examples of the similarity of thought between Paul and users of contemporary friendship language.[39] For example, unity is a fruit of the Spirit and evidence of the Spirit's activity. Paul appeals for unity and its demonstration within the congregation. He says,

> [Whether I come or am absent] I will know that you are standing firm in one spirit, striving side by side with one mind for the faith of the gospel. . . . And this is God's doing. (1:27-28b)

Fitzgerald marks these expressions, among others, as typical of contemporary extra-biblical friendship language. Also in Paul's words "striving side by side with one mind (*mia psychē*)" (1:27) and "being of the same mind" (2:2; 4:2), he sees the proverbial saying, "friends have all things in common," reflected. He says, "Paul's emphasis on sharing in his letter to the Philippians should be seen, at least in part, in the light of this ancient definition of friendship in terms of *koinōnia*."[40]

The reception of gifts from the Philippians requires special attention. Ken Berry contributes to the identification of Paul's language with contemporary friendship language. He studies Philippians 4:10-20 and says concerning the gift, "[It] was a sign of their spiritual fellowship or unity with Paul and their desire to be present with him."[41] He says, "In 2:1 Paul appeals to unity and harmony on the basis of their experience of *koinōnia pneumatos,* i.e. either their 'joint-participation' in the Spirit or their 'fellowship' created by the Spirit."[42] Berry also notes that for Paul this relationship was not based on personal gain and that,

---

38. Malherbe, "Paul's Self-Sufficiency," 138.

39. John T. Fitzgerald, "Philippians in the Light of Some Ancient Discussions of Friendship," in Fitzgerald (ed.), *Friendship* (above, note 36), 141-60 .

40. *Ibid.,* 146. See also Ken L. Berry, "The Function of Friendship Language in Philippians 4:10-20," 107-24.

41. Ken L. Berry, "The Function of Friendship Language in Philippians 4:10-20," 117.

42. *Ibid.,* 118.

in addition, his independence denied patronage. He emphasizes theological context; he says, "Paul wants the Philippians to see their friendship in the broader context of their relationship to God, to whom their acts of thoughtful concern and generosity are pleasing sacrifices, and who will fulfill all their needs."[43]

G. W. Peterman, independent of the Group, studies extensively the conventional and involved practice of gift giving in the Greco-Roman world. He finds that Paul relied on the Old Testament for including the hand of God in this practice, and he marks differences in customs between Paul and the Greco-Roman world in the exchange.[44] Both in the adaptation of friendship language, and in his indifference to social conventions, Paul demonstrates his independence and the Christianizing of relationships. Peterman finds no indication of an assumption on Paul's part of any social responsibility by his accepting the gift. He writes,

> Instead of an expression of debt or of his intention to repay, the apostle relates his personal reflection, gives moral commendation and offers a theological interpretation of the gift. From this it should be clear that the purpose of Philippians 4:10-20 is not sim-

---

43. *Ibid.,* 123. See also his critique of interpretations of 1:28-31. He says concerning the gift and its significance as it relates to Paul and the Philippians, "I wish to argue that once one recognizes the conventions about friendship with which 4:10-20 is replete, Paul is not roundabout or oblique, nor does he write a thankless thanks, nor is he embarrassed about money matters. What he does, rather, is to draw out, with the aid of such conventions, the significance of the gift as an act by which he and his readers had been drawn more closely together" (130). Malherbe also concentrates his study on the gift from the Philippians. He notes the significance of the reception of the gift as the last item of the letter. He says, "The point is that 4:10-20 is not unique in using friendship language, but is in fact the culmination of a letter that employs such language from the very beginning" ("Paul's Self-Sufficiency," 128).

44. G. W. Peterman, *Paul's Gift from Philippi: Conventions of Gift-Exchange and Christian Giving,* SNTSMS 92 (Cambridge: Cambridge University Press, 1997). In the Greco-Roman world Peterman finds a conventional and involved practice. Social relations were determined by response of receiver to giver. No response indicated enmity, while any response reveals the social status of the two parties. The giver who first gave a gift placed himself in a superior position to the recipient. The relationship might be equalized or reversed by the recipient's gaining advantage in the exchange. At least verbal thanks were expected from the inferior party. See Peterman's Chap. 3, "Giving and Receiving in the Greco-Roman World."

ply to offer a personal response to financial support, but rather to offer instruction on the place of such sharing in the life of the Christian community.[45]

In another collection of studies by the Group, Alan Mitchell has made a detailed study of friendship terminology in Paul, Luke, and John.[46] For Paul's letters he reviews the discussions on the *topos* on friendship found in 1 Thessalonians, Galatians, 1 and 2 Corinthians, Romans, and Philippians. He finds that Paul makes various adaptations of the *topos* to the particular needs of a letter-event. In the complex of friendship or antagonism on the part of the people and his own moods of self-giving or self-sufficiency Mitchell concludes,

> In addressing the needs of these communities, Paul's self-sufficiency emerges as a critical issue. Will he be bound by the conventions of friendship or can he stand free of them in order to preach the gospel as he feels obligated to? Thus if Paul relied on some of the conventions of friendship in order to create communities, he seems also to adjust those conventions in maintaining them. Paul, then, wanted to guide the use of friendship for his purpose, rather than be guided by the conventions of friendship themselves.[47]

This review of the studies of the Group witnesses to the contribution these writers have made to first-century epistolography. They demonstrate Paul's general acquaintance with the contemporary parlance and practice, but are unanimous in acknowledging the apostle's relative independence of them.

---

45. *Ibid.*, 158. In summary fashion Peterman writes, "We have seen the role of gift and service in the Greco-Roman world and though Paul employs the giving and receiving metaphor, the social conventions regarding such relationships are not reflected in Paul's dealing with money in regard to his churches. Paul mentions nothing of any debt which he owes to the Philippians because of the gift he has received" (120).

46. Alan C. Mitchell, S.J., "'Greet the Friends by Name,'" in John T. Fitzgerald (ed.), *Greco-Roman Perspectives on Friendship* (above, note 35), 225-62. See his reviews of the literature.

47. *Ibid.*, 260-61.

3. Conclusion

The verdict of this writer is that Paul was only indirectly and partially influenced by the conventions of personal friendship letters as they formed part of the epistolary milieu in which he lived and wrote. It seems instead that Paul's modes of expression are those of an official speaking within the context of a community in which he is an authority. The following observations support this decision.

Much attention has been given to the avoidance of *philos* and *philia* ("friend" and "friendship," respectively) by Paul. John Reumann makes an extensive review of the literature on friendship tracing its development and offering critiques.[48] In his "Conclusions and Suggestions" he says, "The damaging absence of *philia* terms in Paul has produced several explanations — theologically that *philia* was too anthropocentric for Paul to use [Sevenster]; or sociologically, that Paul desired to avoid the status implications of patronal friendship [Judge]."[49]

This writer suggests that Paul avoided these terms due to connotations they carried in both personal and official letter writing. In personal letters the term *philia* is used chiefly for intimate, person-to-person expressions.[50] Such personalizing was not appropriate for use by an apostle when writing to a corporate group — a congregation —

48. John Reumann, "Philippians, Especially Chapter 4, As a 'Letter of Friendship': Observations on a Checkered History of Scholarship," in Fitzgerald, *Friendship* above, note 36), 88-106.

49. *Ibid.,* 105-6. Alan Mitchell, in commentating on friendship in Rom 16:3:16, says concerning Sevenster, "Sevenster believes Paul's preferred designation, 'fellow workers', tells why he avoids using the words 'friends' or 'friendship.' The bonds of fellow workers who have labored together, perhaps even suffered together for the sake of the gospel, cannot be expressed in terms of friendship" (Alan Mitchell, "'Greet the Friends by Name'" [above, note 35], 233. Mitchell refers to J. N. Sevenster, *Paul and Seneca,* 1961). Concerning Judge, Mitchell says, "E. A. Judge . . . sees the reason in Paul's desire to avoid the status implications of patronal friendship" (259). He also refers to Judge, "Paul's Radical Critic."

50. See Katherine G. Evans, "Friendship in Greek Documentary Papyri and Inscriptions: A Survey," in John T. Fitzgerald (ed.), *Greco-Roman Perspectives on Friendship* (above, note 35), 181-202; see 186-89. Evans' "Survey" supports the evidence from the royal letters. Welles lists eleven uses of *philos* all in the politically restricted sense (Welles, *Royal Cor.* sub index). He says concerning no. 6, line 6, "A king's *philoi* constituted his state council in peace and his general staff in war. At a later time the term became merely a court title" (44). See Welles, no. 14, in Appendix.

and sending general instructions. Here Paul is observing the same social etiquette that he observed when he avoided personal response on the reception of the gift (see Peterman above). In like manner *philos* became a term to designate a member of an officer's staff. Again it is inappropriate for Paul to use in addressing a congregation, and he also avoids it as too specific and formal for addressing his co-workers. In reference to an established relationship between nations *philia* is found twice; *eunoia*, goodwill, is the common word for political friendship between nations.[51]

Paul, therefore, avoids the *philia* terms which have been usurped by other uses less appropriate for his purposes.[52] He uses *philadelphia* occasionally (1 Thess 4:9; Rom 12:10), and *adelphoi* consistently and often. The secretaries' term, *eunoia*, is cooler and more distant; Paul's terms are corporate, warmer, and closer. He chose family terms of "fictive kinship," or, preferably, spiritual kinship, to address the members of the corporate ecclesia. Writers of official letters often wrote to corporate groups, many members of which would not have been personally known to them. Personal letter writers, on the other hand, addressed individuals with whom they were acquainted, in some cases even intimately. The one requires an individualized orientation for expressing friendship; the other, a corporate orientation: Paul's terms favor the corporate address.

In conclusion, as Paul drew upon the whole field of letter writing to create his own apostolic letter, so in this case he reflects acquaintance with the contemporary scene adapting and modifying his expressions of friendly relationships with the churches for his uses. He does so by consecrating his pastoral writings to the service of Christ. In short, Philippians defies classification in either modern or ancient types of friendship letters or letters of affection. It is a joyous letter of thanksgiving, encouragement, and admonition built on *agapē*, divine love, by which the Spirit has bound the apostle and the people in one embrace. In Paul's own words, "And so, my siblings, beloved and longed for, my joy and my crown, stand firm in the Lord, beloved" (4:1).

51. Welles, *Royal Cor.* sub index lists 19 occurrences in 13 letters. He consistently translates, "good will."

52. Notice that Paul does not address even single individuals as friend *(philos)*; e.g. Syzygus (Phil 4:2-3), Epaphroditus (Phil 2:25-30), the acquaintances greeted in Rom 16:3-16, Philemon (2); Philemon is *agapētos, synergos*.

In truth, Paul prepares his own context for his pastoral ministry. In expressing friendship he avoids individual intimacy and verges on official stance as required by the corporate address and the sending of instructions. He prefers the corporate term *adelphoi,* sisters and brothers from the same spiritual womb, recognizing his role as a kind of surrogate parent. As he says, "My little children, for whom I am again in the pain of childbirth until Christ is formed in you . . ." (Gal 4:19). So he places relationships to and within an ecclesia on a higher level than that of social friendships, and he identifies himself in a more authoritative, parental position. He adopts the term *agapē* to represent the divine love due to its dimensions and relations within the divine-human community (Eph 3:18). The depth and extent of the use of this term can be measured from 1 Corinthians 13:1-13 and from its listing in any reliable concordance.

E. Philemon

The letter to Philemon is a striking combination of personal/pastoral and recommendation/official styles. The intent of the letter is very simply the reconciliation of Onesimus and Philemon.[53] As in all Paul's letters, marks of the official stance are apparent. He uses a fitting sender identity, "a prisoner for Christ Jesus"; Eduard Lohse sees a special significance in this appellation:

> [T]he words "a prisoner of Jesus Christ" already indicate that this writing should not be taken to be a mere private letter. It conveys a message that obligates its recipient to obey the apostolic word. The fact that an associate [Timothy] is mentioned also calls attention to the authoritative character of the letter.[54]

53. See Wright's vision of reconciliation in the concept of the people's *koinonia* in Christ through the agency of Paul's ministry. N. T. Wright, "Putting Paul Together Again," in Jouette M. Bassler (ed.), *Pauline Theology Vol. I* (above, note 34), 183-211. For a definitive commentary on Philemon see Joseph A. Fitzmeyer, *The Letter to Philemon,* Anchor Bible (New York: Doubleday, 2000).

54. Lohse well represents the commentators who recognize the official influence on Philm (Eduard Lohse, *Colossians and Philemon,* Hermeneia [Philadelphia: Fortress, 1971]). The citation is from p. 189; see the literature in note 9.

Timothy again serves as co-sender. The letter's intention is to be supported by five fellow workers or greeters; the addressees are multiple: Philemon, two other individuals, and an ecclesia in one of their homes; the ending includes the authenticating autograph (17). Characteristic of the official letter-body are its references to the past (background and basis for the request, 4-7) and present (an appeal, 8-14; a request, 15-20; a conclusion and a final request, 21-22).

The inclusion of the sender's and the recipient's communities again marks Paul's intermediary control and shows that the letter, according to customary protocol, was publicly read. Public reading implied that all parties involved were to be aware of and involved with the business contained in a letter. Thus the second person singular of the body (4-21, to Philemon) is enclosed within the second person plurals of the heading and conclusion (1-3, 23-25, to the ecclesia). And the exchange at the ending turns on v. 22, the request for the guest room (singular) and the request for prayers (plural). In this matter the letter to Philemon is similar to the apostrophe to Syzygus, the yokefellow at Philippi (Phil 4:2-3), and to the treatment of the immoral person at Corinth (1 Cor 5:1-5; cf. Col 4:17). In these incidents Paul holds a congregation responsible for complying with his requests.

Within these epistolary characteristics Paul makes use of subtly persuasive language. For example, he disguises his authoritative office. He strengthens the rhetorical figure of the simple form, "I need not say that . . . ," with the extended statement,

> For this reason though I am bold enough in Christ to command you to do your duty, yet I would rather appeal to you on the basis of love — and I, Paul, do this as an old man and now also as a prisoner of Jesus Christ. (8-9; cf. 2 Cor 8:8)

His authority is implied in the verb "send," and the sending includes a part of his own person, his very heart. He says concerning Onesimus, "I am sending him, that is, my own heart back to you" (12).

Lohse offers a detailed analysis and an exemplary commentary on Paul's finely wrought "intercession for Onesimus."[55] And Andrew Wil-

---

55. Eduard Lohse, *Colossians and Philemon* (preceding note), 196-205. See Fitzmeyer's survey of the "Occasion" of the letter, *The Letter to Philemon* (above, note 53), 17-23; F. Forrester Church, "Rhetorical Structure and Design in Paul's Letter to Philemon," *HTR* 17

son offers a treatment of Paul's strategies of politeness. Wilson concludes,

> We have also seen expressed through these strategies the complex relationship which exists between Paul and Philemon in this social situation. As the apostle of Christ, Paul has the authority to direct the church and its members, but at the same time he shows considerable respect for Philemon's face in front of the church at Colossae.[56]

The letter to Philemon reveals Paul's matured mastery of letter writing as a medium for his ministry. He has melded a professional authority with the affection of his deeply pastoral heart. He clothes authority with expressions of affection, and he does so having mastered the forms, both personal and official, which will enable him to express himself persuasively.

Letters of recommendation or introduction bind the individuals involved in the letter-event closely together.[57] In this letter Paul relies on the intimate relationships within the social circle of this house church. The letter unites Paul and the community with him, Philemon and the community with him, and both with Onesimus. As noted above, here in a short letter, Paul conducts a ministry of reconciliation similar to

---

(1968): 17-33. Church compares Phlm to a deliberative speech. See his notes and bibliography. S. B. C. Winter, "Methodological Observations on a New Interpretation of Paul's Letter to Philemon," *USQR* 39 (1984): 203-12. Winter argues that the letter was sent to Archippus in whose house the congregation convened. Philemon and Apphia were members and would preside over the business regarding Onesimus. Onesimus had been sent to serve Paul, and now Paul asks that he be manumitted to serve the church in a new social and legal status.

56. Andrew Wilson, "The Pragmatics of Politeness and Pauline Epistolography: A Case Study of the Letter to Philemon," *JSNT* 48 (1992): 107-19. The quotation is from p. 118.

57. Letters of recommendation vary in expression according to the degree of intimacy among the parties. Furnish describes two categories. He observes, "Such letters of introduction, whether official (certifying someone as a duly commissioned representative or messenger of another) or unofficial (commending a relative, friend, or associate of another), played a larger role in the ancient world . . ." (Victor Paul Furnish, *II Cor.* [above, note 32], 193). Socrates *Ep.* 28 is a letter of recommendation exchanged between representatives of high officialdom. Even a quick reading reveals Paul's melding of an authoritative position with his deep pastoral concerns.

that in reconciling Euodia and Syntyche and dealing with the immoral individual at Corinth.

E. J. Goodspeed, referring to James Stalker, wrote, "Doctor Stalker once said that the letters of Paul take the roofs off the meeting places of the early Christians and let us look inside."[58] This writer is pleased to indulge in such an imaginary view. The drama of the setting enhances the event. As the one recommended, Onesimus carries the letter to be read before the ecclesia, certainly by Archippus if not by Philemon himself. The surprise created by Onesimus' return, the temerity of his presentation of the letter, the summoning of a meeting, and the tension of awaiting Philemon's response all create a drama the denouement of which we can only surmise.

F. Galatians

1. The "Brothers" as the Delegation from Galatia

The marks of the official letter on Galatians are a strong sender identity, the inclusion of co-senders, the absence of a thanksgiving, the dual body elements, and the subscription.

The salutation, "the whole group of brothers with me," is a unique address, found only here; the other letters (excepting Romans) name individuals as co-senders. The identity of these brothers becomes, therefore, a key to interpreting the letter. A number of suggestions have been made; they are, however, highly speculative. The brothers could be the congregation at the place from which Paul is writing. Or they may be the Relief Fund trustees with whom Paul has chanced to meet, or some other group of travelers also met by chance. Another suggestion based on something more than speculation can be gained from certain considerations, however: it is the conclusion of this writer that the brothers are a delegation to Paul from Galatia. This conclusion is derived from identifying the purpose for which Paul uses co-senders and from the influence of official letter writing, specifically the similarities of salutations on his letters with those on other official letters. Some

---

58. Edgar J. Goodspeed, *An Introduction to the New Testament* (Chicago: University of Chicago Press, 1937), 39.

observations concerning the phrasing of this salutation corroborate this hypothesis.

As demonstrated in Chapter II, the naming of co-senders is a convention in official correspondence, especially that of intermediate officials who name colleagues or visiting envoys.[59] And this type of official letter, as we have seen, is especially helpful for interpreting Paul's letters. The apostle usually follows the convention of naming individual co-senders; in this letter he does not. Nor does he name them elsewhere in the letter. Yet we know from the letters in which co-senders are named that they play an important role in the initiation and the content of the letters. Timothy, for example, reports to Paul on the situations in Thessalonica and Corinth; he is to follow Paul's letter to Philippi, and he is with Paul when he makes the decision about Onesimus. Silvanus, too, is with Paul and can testify to Paul's anxiety while awaiting word from the Thessalonians. From these examples it seems evident that Paul does not name as co-senders people only temporarily or peripherally connected with a letter-event. The same, then, should be assumed for the brothers.

Thus two suggestions concerning the identity of the brothers can be dismissed. The reference cannot be to the local congregation from which Paul is writing, nor is it to travelers who have chanced to meet with Paul at Corinth. The former suggestion is that of Wm. M. Ramsay.[60] From

---

59. For this paragraph see Chapter II, "The Official Letter-Form and the Pauline Letters."

60. Wm. M. Ramsay, *A Historical Commentary on St. Paul's Epistle to the Galatians* (New York, 1900; Grand Rapids: Baker, 1965), 242-44. Phil 4:21a, *hoi syn emoi adelphoi,* merits special comment. The phrase in the salutation, "to all the saints" (1:1), and the phrase in the greeting, "greet every saint" (4:21a), are addressed by Paul (and Timothy) to the whole congregation in Philippi. But what is the relation of the two phrases identifying the people at the place of writing who send greetings to Philippi? The phrases are: *hoi syn emoi adelphoi* of 4:21b and *pantes hoi hagioi* of 4:22. There are two possibilities. (1) The phrases are in apposition: "The brothers and sisters with me [i.e., the congregation at the place of writing] greet you, I mean, all the saints greet you, especially those of Caesar's household." Or, (2) "The brothers and sisters with me [i.e., some group not otherwise designated] greet you; in addition all the saints of the congregation here greet you, especially those of Caesar's household." Note that with (2) even without *pantes* (hardly needed here — the Philippians would know to what kind of a group Paul refers), "the brothers and sisters with me," as in the case of Gal, designates some group, some delegation with Paul, certainly in this letter, from Philippi.

Philippians he cites *tois hagiois* (1:1) and *hoi syn emoi adelphoi* (4:21, cf. 22) to show that *adelphoi* like *hagioi* may refer to the congregation. This is true, but *adelphoi* is also used by Paul for a limited group apart from a congregation (see below). And in view of Paul's practice of using people involved in the letter-event as co-senders, a limited number of participating brothers is indicated for the Galatian salutation. For the same reason, J. B. Lightfoot's suggestion that the brothers are travelers who have chanced to meet with Paul at Corinth cannot identify the brothers.[61] In both of these suggested identities the brothers could be only peripherally involved in the letter-event and would not have satisfied the requirements for serving as co-senders in what is clearly an intense and critical event.

There are two remaining possibilities: either they are members of the Famine Relief Commission,[62] or they are a delegation from Galatia who have come to consult with Paul. That they are members of the Relief Commission may be dismissed for a number of reasons. Paul is committed to the Relief Fund and enthusiastic about it. He asks for prayers in support of that mission (Rom 15:30-32); he highly commends the churches of Macedonia for their generous participation in it (2 Cor 8:1-2) and urges the Corinthians to follow their example (9:1-5). He has formerly given specific directions to the churches in Galatia for the collecting of their offering and repeats the same to the Corinthians (1 Cor 16:1-4). Now in writing to Galatia he makes no mention of these directives. In view of his enthusiasm and on the supposition that the brothers are trustees of the Relief Fund, it is difficult to imagine that either before or after a contribution to that fund by the Galatians no mention would be made of it. Could Paul be anticipating the trip to Jerusalem in the presence of these brothers dedicated to that cause and not in some way commend them or refer to the business in which they were engaged? Would the Galatians' interest or lack of interest go unmentioned and not be used to illustrate freedom and its exercise in love apart from the law (Gal 5:13-15)? Would it not come to mind when Paul speaks of doing good to those of the household of faith (Gal 6:9-10)? Would it not be of significance when he recalls other visits to Jerusalem

61. J. B. Lightfoot, *The Epistle of St. Paul to the Galatians* (London, 1890; Grand Rapids, Zondervan, 1957), note on 1:2.

62. Werner Foerster, "Abfassungszeit und Ziel des Galaterbriefes," in W. Eltester and F. H. Kettler (eds.), *Apophoreta: Festschrift für Ernst Haenchen* (Berlin: Töpelmann, 1964), 135-41.

and the admonition of the "pillars" to remember the poor (Gal 2:10)? The absence of even an indirect reference to the fund, its trustees, or the mission to Jerusalem, indicates that Paul does not have in mind the fund or the Galatians' contribution to it. It is impossible to imagine that Paul would be in the presence of trustees of the Relief Fund, or be traveling with them, and disregard their mission entirely while using them as co-senders in writing to Galatia on subjects not directly relevant to them. If they were trustees of the fund they might send greetings at the end of the letter; they would not be named as co-senders.[63] It must be concluded that the brothers are not involved in any way with that undertaking.

By process of elimination one identification remains: the brothers are a delegation from Galatia. In addition to the arguments above, some observations concerning the wording of the salutation are pertinent and support this conclusion. The salutation reads,

Paulus . . . kai hoi syn emoi pantes adelphoi . . .

Paul . . . and the whole group of brothers with me . . .

Paul's use of *pas* is of first significance.[64] Of the many occurrences, five including the Galatian salutation and one in which the noun is supplied from the context are written in the complete attributive phrase

---

63. Identifying the brothers with the Fund has provided a key to the dating of Gal (Funk et al.). Denying that identification opens the problem again. Why is there no mention of the project even when opportunities were present as listed above? Dismissing the remote possibility that the letter was written before the famine in Jerusalem, the answer must be that the brothers are not trustees and Paul was so deeply preoccupied with the problems at Galatia verging on the near apostasy of the people, that he wrote of nothing else. The letter is an official, apostolic communication directed to the denunciation of heterodoxy.

64. Of the more than three hundred occurrences of the word, twenty-six are in the attributive position. Of these, twenty-one are substantive. The five complete attributive phrases are: "Within the congregation, if all bodily members as a whole were one member, what would become of the body?" (1 Cor 12:19, *ei de ēn ta panta [melē] hen melos . . .*). "'The sum total of us' (Moulton-Turner) must appear before the judgment seat of Christ . . ." (2 Cor 5:10, *tous gar pantas hēmas*). "Greet Philologus . . . and Olympas, and all the saints who are with them" (Rom 16:15, *tous syn autois pantas hagious*). "The whole law is summed up in a single commandment" (Gal 5:14, *ho gar pas nomos . . .*). "The whole group of brothers with me" (Gal 1:1).

(article, modifier, substantive) and show the significance of this position.[65] These phrases and the contexts define the unity and identity of a group, collection, assemblage, as a whole. The reference is not to individual people or things constituting a group and being indefinite in number or identity.[66] The brothers are a definable, identifiable group. Hans Dieter Betz summarizes this use succinctly:

> Paul does not name them [the brothers], but we can assume that he refers to fellow missionaries known to the Galatians, and not from the whole church from where he sent the letter. The emphatic 'all' is unique in Paul and indicates that he wanted to write as the spokesman of a group which is solidly behind him and the letter.[67]

However, "fellow missionaries" would seem to refer to a chance meeting, not to a delegation from Galatia. Such a delegation would more likely be "solidly behind him and the letter."

The choice of the preposition *syn* adds to the limitation imposed by the attributive position of *pas* and indicates a close bond between the brothers and Paul. He uses *syn* and its variants thirty times in the seven letters. Eleven times it occurs in the phrase "with Christ" and related phrases, or in describing reunion at the resurrection.[68] Four times it describes accompanying circumstances, all of which are referred to divine activity.[69] The remaining fifteen acknowledge mutual relationships in a letter-event or in other ministries.[70] In Pauline use the prepo-

---

65. The statistics in this section are listed for the seven uncontested letters and taken from K. Aland (ed.), *Vollstandige Konkordanz* (Berlin: de Gruyter, 1980). In the attributive uses as substantives, the neuter *(panta)* occurs fifteen times and the masculine *(pantes* personal) six times. In the latter cases the noun is not supplied from the context, and they are, therefore, listed as substantives. In the attributive position as adjectival (the complete phrase), *pas* occurs five times as listed in the preceding note.

66. See James Hope Moulton and Nigel Turner, *A Grammar of New Testament Greek*, Vol. III (Edinburgh: T&T Clark, 1963), 199-201; BDF 275 (I), (7); *TDNT* s.v. *pas*, V 887 (Reicke).

67. Hans Dieter Betz, *Galatians: A Commentary on Paul's Letter to the Churches in Galatia* (Philadelphia: Fortress, 1979), 40. See the references in his notes.

68. Rom 6:8; 8:32; 2 Cor 1:21; 4:14 bis; 13:4; Phil 1:23; 1 Thess 4:14, 17 bis; 5:10.

69. 1 Cor 10:13; 11:32; Gal 3:9; 5:24.

70. In a letter-event: the salutation designating co-senders, Gal 1:2. Salutations desig-

sition involves people in the divine fellowship or unites them with one another in communication either by letter or in apostolic mission. In the latter cases the association is specifically with Paul and under his direction.[71]

The use of *syn* and the position of *pas* unite to define a limited group of brothers who are present with Paul; and, as is Paul's custom in the naming of co-senders, it is concluded that they are participants in the letter-event.

As for *adelphoi,* in the New Testament the word generally denotes Christians, believers, especially the corporate membership of a congregation. However, Paul also uses the term to identify a group apart from a congregation or from believers in general.[72] The restricted use of *adelphoi* may also have reference to people on mission.[73]

---

nating recipients, 1 Cor 1:2; 2 Cor 1:1; Phil 1:1. Greetings, Rom 16:14, 15; 1 Cor 16:19; Phil 4:21. In other ministries *(syn emoi):* the Corinthian members of the Relief Commission, 1 Cor 16:4; an unnamed person identified with the Relief Commission, 2 Cor 8:19 (see variant); a group of Macedonians, 2 Cor 9:4. Timothy as a fellow servant, Phil 2:22-23; Titus, Gal 2:3. The power of the Lord Jesus, 1 Cor 5:4. The grace of God, 1 Cor 15:10 (variant).

71. The preposition *meta* meaning "with" occurs forty-one times in the seven letters. In contrast to *syn,* twenty-five times it is used with liturgical or affective expression; ten times meaning to live, be, share, contend with, someone; once in an OT quotation. Five times it approaches Paul's use of *syn* in reference to people coming, going, sent (1 Cor 16:11, 12; 2 Cor 8:18; Gal 2:1), or being co-workers (Clement with Euodia and Syntyche, Phil 4:13). These five phrases unite people in ministries in which Paul is not immediately involved or for which he does not take full responsibility. He disassociates himself by using *meta* for the association of others and *syn* for his own direct involvement either in person or by letter. On this understanding of the two prepositions Titus is Paul's colleague at the Jerusalem meeting *(ho syn emoi,* Gal 2:3), while Barnabas accompanies them independently *(meta,* 2:1).

72. See references in *TDNT,* s.v. *adelphos* (von Soden); and 2 Macc 1:1; Acts 15:23; 1 Cor 16 *passim;* Arland J. Hultgren, "The Self-Definition of Paul and His Communities," *SEÅ* 56 (Uppsala, 1991), 78-100; see 93-95. Ellis refers to ". . . texts in which *hoi adelphoi* appears to be used along side of and in distinction from the church as a whole." Two of these texts ". . . clearly imply that 'the brothers' are a more restricted group than 'the Christians,' i.e., *hoi hagioi, hai ekklesiai*" (E. Earle Ellis, "Paul and His Co-Workers," *JTS* 17 [1970-71]: 446). The two texts are 1 Cor 16:19-20 and Phil 4:21-22.

73. For example, in the chapters on the Relief Fund (2 Cor 8-9) two brothers are making the trip. One is well known to the churches and has previously been elected to serve on the Relief Commission (2 Cor 8:18-19); the other has a special concern for the Corinthians (2 Cor 8:22). They are emissaries who represent their respective churches (2 Cor 8:23). Also in 1 Corinthians 16 are references identifying brothers with people on

The reception of envoys from sending communities is elsewhere noted in official letter writing. They are sometimes referred to with the phrase, *hoi syn autōi*. The following examples occur in the correspondence between Jonathan and Josephus. This selection is an account of Josephus' dealing with an embassy led by Jonathan and sent from Jerusalem under authorization of Simon and Ananias, the high priest, to remove Josephus from the command in Galilee and to install Jonathan in his place. Three letters were exchanged:

Jonathan and those with him [*hoi syn autōi*] sent from the Jerusalemites to Josephus greeting. *(Life 217)*

Josephus to Jonathan and those with him [*tois syn autōi*] greeting. *(Ibid., 226)*

Jonathan and those with him [*hoi syn autōi*] to Josephus greeting. *(Ibid., 229)*[74]

---

mission. Timothy is on his way to Corinth. Paul along with *(meta)* the brothers awaits his return (1 Cor 16:10-11). Also, Paul urges Apollos to go to Corinth with *(meta)* the brothers; and he has received the three men from Corinth (1 Cor 16:17). In these chapters Titus is not designated brother. He is going because of Paul's appeal to him and of his own accord. His zeal for the Corinthians is inspired by God; he is not being sent by Paul (2 Cor 8:16-17). He is "my partner and co-worker on your behalf" (v. 23). Paul implies that Titus represents him personally and not one of the congregations, and that the delegation is under Titus' leadership. This delegation does not appear to be the full and final commission; it is a special group going to Corinth for that and other purposes. It is not possible to determine how these references are related to one another, or to how many groups they refer. It is clear that the term "brothers" is used in reference to a restricted group (or groups) small enough in number to travel back and forth to Corinth or to pass through the city on some mission. Notice that Paul's use of *meta* disassociates himself and Apollos from any close involvement in these situations. Other uses of "brother(s)" with verbs of sending or coming: Timothy, 1 Thess 3:2, see 1 Cor 4:7; Titus, 2 Cor 2:13, see 12:18, Gal 2:3; Epaphroditus, Phil 2:25 (note synonyms with "brother"). See also 2 Cor 11:9; Col 4:7-9; Acts 28:21; Ellis (preceding note), 447.

74. See also *PTebt* 382, line 20; Polycarp to the Philippians *(kai hoi syn autōi presbyteroi)*; Ps. Ignatius to St. John *(et qui cum eo sunt fratres)*. Also it should be noted, Paul uses the first person, "with me," not, as is customary in official letters, the third person "with him" referring to the writer. Paul does not refer to himself in the third person. The only other use of the first person referring to the writer in the salutation and known to me is the use in personal letters with *kurios, kuria* (my lord, my lady). *POxy* 1770 (Exler, no. 14, p. 34; see other examples on pp. 33-35).

The *hoi syn autōi* refers to official emissaries attending Jonathan. Their official status is made clear in the first reference by the participial phrase, "sent by the Jerusalemites." In the movements of the envoys the identifying phrase is not repeated in the subsequent references. An explanation may be that Josephus added the words editorially at the first reference for a clarification for the general reader, and they are not repeated. Or having once introduced the emissaries, the original writer or Josephus did not think it necessary to repeat the phrase. It would be awkward for Josephus to use it. Paul does not use any identifying phrase. He is writing to a limited circle of recipients to whom the co-senders, participants in the letter-event, are well known. Josephus is writing to unlimited readers of his history.

It must be noted that, although the reports from Corinth have been brought to Paul by Chloe's people (1 Cor 1:11; 7:1), Paul does not include them as co-senders in the way in which he recognizes the delegation from Galatia. An explanation may be found in the different status of the two groups. The one identified with Chloe may too easily be identified with a faction and, therefore, not represent the whole assembly; the other from Galatia was authorized by the church. Whatever the factional loyalties of the members of Chloe's group might have been, they certainly included supporters of Paul. By not naming them as co-senders Paul withheld formal recognition, and thus he avoided any possible show of favoritism toward individuals or factions. On the other hand the delegates from Galatia were of such a status as to be recognized as official emissaries appointed by the churches, a status that Paul acknowledged by including them in the office of co-senders.

A possible setting for the total letter-event is suggested after the comparison of Galatians with a letter from Antigonus to Scepsis.

2. Galatians and a Letter from Antigonus to Scepsis

Parallels between Paul's letter to the Galatians and Antigonus' letter to Scepsis (Welles, no. 1) can help us to imagine a setting that provides a context for this crucial event. Similarities in form and function might also be found in a comparison, but for this section on Galatians the comparison is used to suggest a reconstruction of the meeting with the Galatian delegation. The reconstruction helps to visualize the initiation and the summoning of the conference, the role of participants, the protocol, the agenda, and the intensity of spirit. Interestingly, both letters represent turning points in Western history — the one political, the other religious. The people of Antigonus' letter are all former "friends" of Alexander and now inimical contestants for all or part of his empire. The letter reports on the peace of 311 BCE, by which a temporary settlement for the division of the empire was reached between Antigonus and a coalition of Lysimachus and Ptolemy. Antigonus had striven for a larger and more prestigious share, but settled with the others by centering his interests on Greece and claiming to be the protagonist of freedom for them. The letter is a report to Scepsis regarding Antigonus' part in developing the treaty of peace and his encouragement for the city to join the movement. Paul's letter, on the other hand, documents the division of primitive Christianity and the struggles resulting therefrom. It also represents a crucial turn in the history of Western Christianity.

The general theme of both letters is the securing of freedom. Antigonus' concern is for the truce that promised the Greek cities their independence. Paul's struggle is for the independence of the Gentile churches. Antigonus announces that peace with Cassander and the others has been made, and therefore encourages Scepsis to join in the peace movement by taking an oath. Paul recounts the agreement with Peter, James, and John, and therefore insists on freedom of the Gentiles from the ritual requirements of Torah. Both writers have attended a major conference with representatives of the opposing position. Subsequent negotiations have been made through envoys or with the chief participants in person. The exchange of documents is recorded by Antigonus but not by Paul; the letter he is sending is the document (cf. Acts 15:22ff.).

As for the terms, Antigonus had been under the impression that his opportunities (ambitions) were limited, but at least the treaty was favorable to the Greeks. Paul had thought that he and the pillars had reached full understanding for the division of their ministries. Both record being certain of the terms. The breach of agreements is the cause of confusion and trouble. In both cases there is early "outside" interference, but strong, current, opposition in Galatia is Paul's major concern. Breach of the treaty is yet to come among the successors of Alexander.

Antigonus gives short, pointed reasons for his settlement with the other generals. Final disposition of the letter on stone limits the length. Paul, on the other hand, is free to list his arguments at length and does so.

Personal participation of each writer can be seen in the letters' preparation. Welles notes, "There is a fine personal touch in the expression *eph' hēmon,* here [l. 21], and in line 56" (p. 10). Antigonus wrote, ". . . we were anxious that the question of the Greeks be setttled in our lifetime" (l. 21). And in the note on line 65 (p. 10) Welles says, "Here and below in line 69, only, Antigonus uses the singular *(moi).* In both cases it is an expression of his personal opinion . . . he distinguishes between himself as an individual and as the representative of a state" (p. 10). He summarizes, "[The letter] has clearly the personal stamp. . . . If it was not the personal composition of Antigonus himself, it was undoubtedly written under his direction and subject to his correction" (p. 11). Antigonus' relationship with a particular city is much less intimate than Paul's relationship with his churches. In Paul's more intimate relationship, the first person singular appears throughout and with strong expressions. For example,

> I am astonished that you are so quickly deserting the one who called you. (1:6)

> I received it [the gospel] through a revelation of Jesus Christ. (1:12b)

> But when Cephas came to Antioch, I opposed him to his face. (2:11)

> Friends, I beg you to become as I am, for I also have become as you are. (4:12)

> Listen! I, Paul, am telling you. (5:2)

In addition to the personal touch an apologetic note is evident in both letters. Such is the case when an historical review is narrated by a person deeply involved and deeply invested in persuading the recipients to accept the advantages procured by the history he has reviewed. Antigonus writes concerning his efforts,

> What zeal we have shown in these matters will I think be evident to you and to all others from the settlement itself. (ll. 24-26)

And concerning the truce with Ptolemy,

> We saw that it was no small thing to give up part of an ambition for which we had taken no little trouble and incurred much expense. Nevertheless [for reasons listed] we thought it was well to yield and to make the truce with him also. (ll. 32-46; see reference to personal touch above)

Paul writes in his introductory declaration,

> Am I now seeking human approval, or God's approval? (1:10)

> But when God . . . was pleased to reveal his Son to me . . . I did not confer with any human being, nor did I go up to Jerusalem. (1:15-17)

The apologetic note pervades 2:1-14. For example,

> I went up [to Jerusalem] in response to a revelation. Then I laid before them . . . the gospel that I proclaimed among the Gentiles, in order to make sure that I was not running, or had not run, in vain. (2:2)

And in the subscription with concluding finality,

> May I never boast of anything but the cross of our Lord Jesus Christ, by which the world has been crucified to me, and I to the world. (6:14)

> From now on, let no one make trouble for me; for I carry the marks of Jesus branded on my body. (6:17)

In both letters the background sections contain underlying personal and apologetic themes. These themes also serve the ultimate purpose of the letters. That is, the background in both communications lays the ground and gives the reasons for the recipients' compliance with the overall purpose of the writing. For Antigonus the purpose is to persuade the people to join in the peace he has procured for them; for Paul, to arouse the people to realize and exercise the freedom he has obtained for them.

Finally, Welles says concerning the destination of Antigonus' letter,

> The letter is not a special communication to Scepsis. Nothing, except the heading and the name of the envoy at the end, need have been changed before it could have been sent to any other Greek city. Undoubtedly copies of it were sent out widely; otherwise a town of the comparative insignificance of Scepsis would hardly have received one. It was intended to be read throughout the Greek world, and everywhere to win public opinion for Antigonus. (p. 11)

In comparison with Antigonus' broad political stroke, Paul's view of the function and destination of his letter was more limited. It was to be read to the churches of Galatia in order to settle an ecclesiastical dispute. However, Welles' setting of Antigonus' letter and the identification of the brothers as a delegation from Galatia suggest a reconstruction of the Galatian letter-event. Allowing for the imaginative reconstruction, it offers, nevertheless, a context that will account for Paul's emotional distress and the strong language in which it is expressed.[75] The letter requires some such context.

A strong stimulus has elicited the response to Galatia in this heart-rending, heated letter. It would have been brought and discussed by a group well informed and deeply concerned by the situation.

As stated above, the silence in which Paul usually encloses his co-senders extends even to the naming of the brothers from Galatia. However, as co-senders they are recognized as official representatives of the churches of Galatia. They are responsible for initiating the conference, bringing the agenda, participating in the discussion, aiding in preparing the epistolary record, and delivering it to their churches. They are well known.

Paul has met with the brothers from Galatia. There is no mention that they brought a written report from Galatia, no need for a seriatim reply as in the case of Corinth. Paul himself was unable or unwilling to visit the churches, even preferring to respond by letter. A conference

---

75. For example: emphatic statements, Listen! I, Paul, am telling you . . . (5:2); I wish those who unsettle you would castrate themselves! (5:12; cf. 1:6-9; 2:14b [to Peter]); argumentative review of history (1:11–2:14) and supportive arguments from OT (3:6-18; 4:21–5:1); interspersed questions, The only thing I want to learn from you is this: Did you receive the Spirit by doing the works of the law or by believing what you heard? (3:2; cf. 3:1-5); Why then the law? (3:19).

was held; this was no short meeting. One must imagine lengthy presentations and discussions under Paul's strong participation. The autographic subscription shows that at least for the validation of this letter Paul took the pen in hand; for what other sections he may have done the same cannot be determined (cf. Gal 5:2). One can imagine that Paul, addressing the churches, dictated major parts of the letter after formulating the responses during and at the end of the conference. No final revision was necessary; the brothers would tend to that. The letter was entrusted to them and to their use of it.

The presence of the emissaries, the preparation of the letter in some such manner, and its significance, make of the whole an authorized report of the conference between Paul and the emissaries to be delivered to the troubled churches. The emissaries' reports to their home churches must be left unrecorded. It was a part of their office to deliver oral messages along with the letters. They took over the responsibility for delivery, presentation to the several churches, and the interpretation of any portion of the letter. They probably delivered and read it in company together as in the reports from the Jerusalem Council (Acts 15:22-35). They knew Paul's tone and mood. They were well acquainted with the content, intent, and rhetorical force of the letter. They knew it to be Paul's personal privilege to make an addendum to accounts of the Jerusalem Council.

This setting offers a context for the source of Paul's information brought by the delegates from Galatia. It is a vital setting large enough to accommodate this deeply disturbing occasion. It is a setting large enough to account for the strong language often observed and reported. Such a record comes from an original actual occasion as if reported live on videotape. Some of the rhetoric may not have been spoken to imaginary opponents; some opponents may have been present at the meeting or even in the delegation. History and apology would be called forth by the discussions. Questions were give and take. The mood and spirit of the meeting are embodied in the report.

For Paul the use of letter writing and his own confidence in the medium have grown and matured from 1 Thessalonians in hesitant, written answer to Timothy's report, to 1 Corinthians when he receives Chloe's delegation, to the expression of *agapē* to the Philippians, to the finely wrought appeal to Philemon, and now this masterly response to wayward churches. Paul develops his apostolic letter even further; he transcends the normative forms to write the letter addressed to Romans.

G. The Letter to the Romans and the Letter-Essay[76]

The emphasis of this study so far has been to delineate Paul's use of the normative forms of Greek letter writing and his mastery and creative adaptation of them for his own unique settings. Special attention has been given to the influence of the official letter. But for the classification of Romans a broader field of activity must be considered. In his epistolary communication Paul was highly creative, drawing upon all types widely used in contemporary communications: the personal letter, the official letter, and, especially in Romans, the letter-essay. It is the limited intention of this section to show that for Romans Paul reflects the setting of the letter-essay.[77]

Joseph Fitzmyer applies the extended concept of the addressees, a characteristic of the letter-essay that Donfried notes, in Romans. He sees the triangular field of recipients behind Paul's purposes in writing to Rome but prefers to reverse the hyphenated term letter-essay to essay-letter. He writes,

> It [the essay-letter] was destined for particular addressees and treated a specific topic, but it was intended to be read by others

76. See the major studies of this letter. E.g., David M. Hay and E. Elizabeth Johnson (eds.), *Pauline Theology Volume III: Romans* (Minneapolis: Fortress, 1995). For the problems confronting the interpreter of this letter, see Leander E. Keck, "What Makes Romans Tick?" in *ibid.*, 3-29; see Robert Jewett, "Ecumenical Theology for the Sake of Mission," esp. his "brief treatment of the rhetoric of Romans," in *ibid.*, 91-93, and his collected bibliography, 301-29.

77. When I first offered the study on the letter-essay to the SBL Epistolography Seminar, I did not have in mind any one of Paul's letters. The intention was to describe this extended letter-form in its ancient uses. Only casual thought was given to its applicability to Paul's letters. Karl Donfried saw that the study has bearing on Romans (Karl P. Donfried, "False Presuppositions in the Study of Romans," in Donfried [ed.], *The Romans Debate*, revised and expanded edition [Peabody, MA: Hendrickson, 1991], 102-27; see esp. 121-25). Stirewalt, "The Form and Function of the Greek Letter-Essay," in *ibid.*, 147-71). Fitzmyer applies to Romans the conception of the dual type of address customary in letter-essays (Joseph A. Fitzmyer, *Romans: A New Translation with Introduction and Commentary*, The Anchor Bible [New York: Doubleday, 1993], see esp. 68-69). It seems appropriate now to follow up on these insights. See Bauckham's critique and his suggestion that the Apocryphon of James fits the type of letter-essay (Richard Bauckham, "Pseudo-Apostolic Letters," *JBL* 107 [1988]: 469-94). The similarities and differences between Paul's letters and the letter-essay are noted below.

than the addressees. This description fits Romans rather well in my opinion, even though I should prefer to label it an "essay-letter," to put stress on its missive character, an aspect that the German term "Lehrbrief" (didactic letter) may better express.[78]

In either wording the emphasis should be put on the epistolary aspect. Paul's letters are "real" letters, written communication between two identifiable parties, in an historical context, on subjects that arise out of their relationships. Paul probably began his letter to Rome to announce his intention to visit the city on his way to Spain. As the conception matured and the realization of the critical juncture in his life and work imposed itself on him, he seized the opportunity to review major topics of his ministry. To this end he tapped into the domain of the letter-essay for some characteristics of form, for the freedom to respond to various topics apart from the immediate demands occasioned by a specific confrontation, and to visualize the addressees in the triangular mode: I/we, you/you all, they. The triangle named the Roman saints, and also reached out to others, perhaps congregations to which the letter might be read in Jerusalem and on the route between Jerusalem and Spain.[79]

It is important at this point to note the differences between Paul's letter to Rome and the letter-essay. The writers of letter-essays are disassociating their writings from oral communication, intending them to be read in more literate academic circles. Paul is writing letters socially and theologically bound to the oral word. He does not conceive of a context in which, on reception, his word is not reanimated by oral speech. He writes, therefore, in a more rhetorically conceived and stylized manner than the letter-essayists wrote. In addition, Paul's personal touches, his expressions of friendship, prayers, and the like, reveal an intimacy not appropriate for the more detached position of the essayist.

From his decade of experience and in anticipation of his trips to Jerusalem, to Rome, and to Spain, Paul had occasion to incorporate elements of the letter-essay into his writing. As with the adaptation of other types, so Romans partakes of the characteristics of form and function of the letter-essay. One does not have to presuppose that Paul was acquainted with the available letter-essays any more than that he

78. Fitzmyer, *Romans* (preceding note), 69.
79. See below, note 86.

was acquainted with the letters of Aristotle and Demetrius' personal letter theories.[80] For the conduct of his epistolary ministry Paul drew upon all forms and functions of written communication, and in his rich creativity forged the apostolic letter. The purpose of the above chapters, to this point, has been to isolate the influence of official letter writing on his communications and meld that with the influence of the personal letter. Now it is appropriate to assess Paul's tapping of the domain of the letter-essay as one of his resources.

Karl Donfried has identified three characteristics of the letter-essay as applicable to Romans: (1) the supplementary purpose of the writing; (2) its publicizing purpose; (3) its intention to instruct.[81] Paul displays evidences of these characteristics in letters written before Romans. The Corinthians have misinterpreted his admonition in a previous letter regarding association with immoral people, and he corrects their misunderstanding and further supports his position.[82] He writes to publicly correct the Philippians in a strongly worded written and recorded statement concerning his understanding of circumcision.[83] Now in his present situation by utilizing the general context and characteristics of the letter-essay he is free to record his thoughts in more reflective contemplation. For example, ever since his conversion Paul has mulled over God's intent for his fellow Jews. Here at last he writes a heart-rending

80. It has been demonstrated that Paul was acquainted with Epicurean thought and therefore, indirectly at least, with its literary expression. It is not inconceivable that Paul knew Epicurus' literary reputation and knew about the medium by which he kept contact with his students, the letter-essay. See esp. Malherbe, *Paul and the Thessalonians* (above, note 2), 101-6.

81. Donfried (ed.), *The Romans Debate* (above, note 77), 123-25, 148. For examples of letter-essays see Stirewalt, "Letter-Essays," in *ibid.,* 148-55.

82. See 1 Cor 5:9-13; cf. 2 Cor 2:2-4, 9, explaining why he wrote as he did; 2 Cor 6:14-7:1, the interpolation reads like a corrective admonition. Paul will clarify for the Galatians and any others that his gospel is the true and only gospel, esp. 1:6-10. Dahl suggests that 1 Cor 5:9ff. may have been written only for clarification (Nils Alstrup Dahl, *Studies in Paul* [above, note 24], 57). Ann Jervis writes concerning 1 Cor 11:2-16, "The position of this study is that in 1 Cor 11:2-16 Paul responds to a misapprehension and consequent misappropriation of his previous teaching on the unity of man and woman in Christ." L. Ann Jervis, "'But I Want You to Know . . .': Paul's Midrashic Intertextual Response to the Corinthian Worshipers (1 Cor 11:2-16)," *JBL* 112 (1993): 231.

83. This strange interruption (Phil 3:1-21?) is variously explained. I suggest it was carried for oral report or on a separate sheet and entrusted to one of the emissaries. A later editor added it indiscriminately.

passage concerning their role in salvation history. He takes the opportunity to record his own internal, lifelong struggle in this fuller response,
and takes the opportunity to review his ministry as consecrated by the
gospel in the life of faith.[84]

The broad, reflective characteristics of the letter-essay are especially pertinent to and evident in Romans. To see the letter-essay type
as part of the setting of Romans, one has only to recognize that at
this juncture of his life Paul was beset from many sources with questions and criticisms of his gospel and instructions. For example, how
did the Galatian churches respond to their letter? What recent reports had been delivered to him that increased his anticipation of a
hostile reception in Jerusalem? Why does his insecurity regarding his
visit to Rome show through in different ways? What reports has he
had, direct and otherwise, from Rome? Now that he is leaving the
area that knows him well, how many problems are unresolved or need
restatement?[85]

Paul faces a critical, crucial point in his life and ministry. His future
is uncertain. He is closing one ministry and planning to open another.
The successes and failures of his work so far bear upon him. His memory is full of recollections of responses by supporters and opponents to
his proclamation, instructions, and pastoral care. Now is the time to
summarize and record in response to the challenges that surround
him. He will address the written word in the first instance to Roman
saints — to that locale which occupies his attention in anticipation of a
new center of mission. But at the same time the message is intended for
all who may hear it. In fact it may be read in Jerusalem and to congregations located en route to Rome.[86]

---

84. E.g. Rom 12:1–15:13, "Paul's Sermon on the Mount."

85. See Dahl's insightful summary of Paul's situation when writing Romans
(Nihls A. Dahl, *Studies in Paul* [above, note 24], 76-77); and Krister Stendahl, *Final Account: Paul's Letter to the Romans* (Minneapolis: Fortress, 1995), 9-20.

86. It might be possible to explain the confusing chap. 16 of Romans as a conflation of
two letters of recommendation for two carriers to introduce each to a congregation en
route. See esp. Harry Gamble, Jr., *The Textual History of the Letter to the Romans: A Study in Textual and Literary Criticism* (Grand Rapids: Eerdmans, 1977), 83; and Norman R. Petersen,
"On the Ending(s) to Paul's Letter to Rome," in B. A. Pearson (ed.), *The Future of Early Christianity: Essays in Honor of Helmut Koester* (Minneapolis: Fortress, 1991), 337-47; see 340-42.
Paul thought of multiple recipients when he wrote to the Galatian churches. He may have

Certain formal characteristics reflect those of the letter-essay. The address is significant: the letter-essay is customarily addressed to one or more individuals who have called forth the response, and also to a general audience of those who have a common interest. In this case the Roman saints are the identified correspondents, and the scattered groups in the east, which Paul is now leaving, share common interests.[87] It is no stretch of the imagination or of Paul's contemporary situation to see the significance of the Roman address and the implication for the broader coverage he has in mind. The imaginary dialogical partners in the letter reveal the broad field. In his mind Paul dialogues with the sinful (2:1-4), with himself (7:14-25, esp. 15), with his brothers and sisters the Jews (9:2-3), with the Gentiles (11:13, 19), and with the Romans (esp. 8:9-17).[88]

Also regarding form, letter-essays are written by a single individual. Paul names no co-sender in Romans. He takes full responsibility for the content, and the closing is not a subscription. It may be that Tertius, on his own, records his role as scribe along with his greeting (16:22). Perhaps he feels that it is part of his official function to make this confirmation of the letter, especially since Paul names no co-sender and does not write a subscription. The letter, like a letter-essay, has no epistolary confirmation.

Paul's disregard of the restrictions concerning the subjects of the

---

recalled that at least two copies of the decision at Jerusalem were prepared, one for each of the two pairs of emissaries (Acts 15). He may have thought in the same way in writing Romans. Neither Gal nor Rom is a "circular letter," i.e. one sent in multiple copies to predetermined locales. Again in the manner of the essayists the third party is implicitly included but not identified. See L. Ann Jervis, *The Purpose of Romans: A Comparative Letter Structure Investigation* (Sheffield: JSOT Press, 1991), 16-17. Among other examples of circular letters see Welles, *Royal Cor.,* no. 1. For references to circular letters, see Stirewalt, *Studies in Ancient Greek Epistolography,* SBLRBS 27 (Atlanta: Scholars Press, 1993), Study IV, "Greek Terms for Letters and Letter-Writing," 80-81.

87. The combination of specific and general address is conventional both for official letters and for letter-essays. In the official letter the specified addressee is usually an intermediary officer with jurisdiction over a well defined political unit which comprises the citizens who, as the general addressees, are directly involved in the message of the letter. In the letter-essay the specified addressee is a correspondent who has made inquiry or criticism. The general audience is an undefined group of people presumed to be interested in the subjects of the communication. Perhaps the essayists borrowed from the officials. Paul's adaptation for Romans is closer to that of the essayists.

88. By the repeated 2nd pers. pl. Paul seems to address chiefly the Romans.

personal and official letters is also evident in the liberties he takes with the letter-essay. He takes advantage of this freedom in writing to the Romans without the pressure of on-the-spot demands. In the manner of the essayists he takes the opportunity to supplement, restate, explain the major subjects that are on his mind. His role of instructor underlies the topics. He does so with the emphasis and in the light and security of his apostolic calling and commissioning. For example, fresh from the Galatian controversy he expands on the relation of law and faith (Rom 2:25–4:25).[89] The problems at Corinth are still on his mind (e.g. Rom 14 and 1 Cor 8), a matter of special significance if the Corinthians are to hear the letter. He will give a didactic application of major themes of the gospel (Rom 1:16–11:36).[90] As already noted, he struggles over the role and salvation of his brothers and sisters, the Jews, in the divine plan. Through it all, instructions are fully seen as the Christian way of life, its hope and divine support consecrated by faith in the gospel (chaps. 8, 9).

The letter to the Romans is a disclosure of Paul's future plans, a spontaneous review of his ministry, and a résumé of his ponderings to date concerning responses to his gospel and to his teachings. It is offered up to the Romans and to all others who may have opportunity to hear it.[91] And it assumes the form of the letter-essay, a document uniquely suited to encompass these purposes.

89. See Fitzmyer's notices of "echoes of themes and phrases from earlier Pauline writings" (*Romans* [above, note 77]), 71-73. Plevnick collects Paul's references to previous positions he has taken (J. Plevnick, "Pauline Presuppositions," in Collins, *Thess. Cor.* [above, note 4], 51-54).

90. N. T. Wright, "Romans and the Theology of Paul," in Hay and Johnson, *Pauline Theology Volume III: Romans* (above, note 76), 30-67; see esp. 34-36, 65-67.

91. See "The Problem of the Purposes of Romans," in L. Ann Jervis, *The Purpose of Romans* (above, note 86), 11-28. She reviews the solutions and the literature.

IV

Paul and His Apostolic, Epistolary Ministry

A. The Significance of the Combination of Epistolary Settings and the Characteristics of Pauline Composition

For the conduct of his epistolary ministry Paul combined the forms and functions of personal and official letter writing. He modified this combination by adapting it to his Christian vision and sense of calling. The significance of the combination of the two basic settings may now be seen.

The adaptation and integration of official letter characteristics undergirded Paul's calling as an intermediary between Christ and the congregation. It enabled him to address the community as community, with the congregation gathered as the primary recipient, the locus of the Spirit's presence, the corporate body that worshipped, confessed, educated, and disciplined together. It allowed him, the sender, to take a more detached position in relation to the recipients, to assume an authoritative office when necessary. It preserved the priority of the spoken word now necessarily or intentionally reduced to writing but reanimated in oral presentation at the social/political level of a community. It commanded respect as the earliest developed and most widely known of the uses of letter writing, the one out of which many and varied uses would grow.[1] It facilitated the publicizing of his message, ad-

1. M. Luther Stirewalt, Jr., *Studies in Ancient Greek Epistolography*, SBLRBS 27 (Atlanta: Scholars Press, 1993). See Study I, "Uses and Development," 6-7.

mitting a triangular setting that visualized third parties, strangers, and visitors (an extension enhanced by the letter-essay).

On the other hand, Paul's adaptation and integration of personal letter characteristics met a number of his other needs. It declared his identification with the people, his commitment to them, and his pastoral concern for them. The personal letter softened the authority and detachment of the imperial model, and it added the warm sensibilities of that medium with which all people were familiar. One function of Paul's letters was to maintain relationships, and in their personal intent they, like the most artful personal letters, were sent as gifts. Their reception expressed Paul's pastoral concern for the people, and by embracing them in the epistolary arm it enhanced their sense of incorporation and worthiness.

This creative combination of characteristics broadened the letter-setting to incorporate all members of Paul's congregations, regardless of their socioeconomic status. Wayne Meeks offers a profile of these congregations: "It is a picture in which people of several social levels are brought together. The extreme top and bottom of the Greco-Roman social scale are missing from the picture." And, "The 'emerging consensus' that Malherbe reports seems to be valid: a Pauline congregation generally reflected a fair cross-section of urban society."[2] Paul's literary innovation and its function maintained and encouraged the continuation of the assemblies of these ordinary people from several different walks of life who might not otherwise have come together.

Although the term "common person" must be more carefully defined in light of the recent studies of Pauline congregations, the study by Eric Auerbach and William Beardslee's comments on it give an insight into Paul's letters. Auerbach shows how the Jewish-Christian reli-

---

2. Wayne A. Meeks, *The First Urban Christians: The Social World of the Apostle Paul* (New Haven: Yale Univ. Press, 1983), see esp. "The Social Level of Pauline Christians," 51-73; citations pp. 72-73. Meeks' reference is to Abraham J. Malherbe, *Social Aspects of Early Christianity* (Philadelphia: Fortress, 1983). For the people of the Pauline congregations see Meeks' full discussion and the literature in the same volume, as well as Jürgen Becker, *Paul: Apostle to the Gentiles* (Louisville: Westminster/John Knox, 1993), 241-44. Doty's "Interpretive Reflections" summarizes the letter-setting (William G. Doty, *Letters in Primitive Christianity* [Philadelphia: Fortress, 1973], 75-76). Botha argues for a low percentage of literate people in the first century (P. J. J. Botha, "Greco-Roman Literacy as Setting for New Testament Writings," *Neot* 26 [1992]: 195-215).

gion overcame the classical disregard for the common people that is so evident in literature.[3] The classic comic and tragic styles demanded as hero — as the one on whom history turned — the uncommon person, superman, superwoman. Auerbach contrasts selections from Petronius' *Banquet* (37f.) and Tacitus' *Histories* (16f.) with Mark's story of Peter's denial. In this connection William Beardslee writes,

> By analyzing these sections, Auerbach shows that the ancient tradition of the separation of the tragic and comic styles was much more than a stylistic convention, and that it expressed a persuasive understanding of reality which prevented both Petronius and Tacitus from taking their common people seriously as vehicles for actual historical transformation. Peter, on the other hand, in Mark's narrative, is engaged in a situation which "sets man's whole world astir," (*Mimesis,* p. 370) which involves the ordinary concrete individual in an emerging historical process and does not reserve serious significance exclusively for the exalted person. . . . Auerbach goes on to comment that the history in question which is coming into being "progresses to somewhere outside of history, to the end of time or the coincidences of all time," (*Ibid.* p. 39) yet from his point of view, what is important is the fact that the concrete ordinary person is presented with utmost seriousness and is taken seriously, not just as an isolated individual, but as a participant in the unfolding reality which compels men's reaction one way or another.[4]

Auerbach and Beardslee are using Mark's narrative to illustrate the Christian regard for the ordinary people who play a crucial role in the drama of history. At least a decade earlier, in the first preserved writ-

---

3. Eric Auerbach, *Mimesis: The Representation of Reality in Western Literature* (Princeton: Princeton University Press, 1953).

4. William A. Beardslee, *Literary Criticism of the New Testament* (Philadelphia: Fortress, 1970), 22-23. Crossan marks the difference by contrasting Caesar Augustus with Jesus of Nazareth and Virgil's Fourth Eclogue with Mark's Gospel (John Dominic Crossan, *Jesus: A Revolutionary Biography* [San Francisco: HarperSanFrancisco, 1994]. See esp. Chap. I). One might also contrast the Monumentum Ancyranum with Mark's Gospel. Tolbert's analysis of the "authorial audience" of Mark's Gospel may be seen as a complementary view of Paul's audience (Mary Ann Tolbert, *Sowing the Gospel: Mark's World in Literary-Historical Perspective* [Minneapolis: Fortress, 1989]).

ings of the church, Paul demonstrated through letter writing the same concern and declared the same good news. The apostolic letter appropriated from official correspondence the care and esteem with which it was written, delivered, and received; receipt of such letters enhanced the sense of worthiness of the recipients. This type of letter recognized the communal authority within a congregation as it was also personified in and articulated by Paul. The apostolic letter appropriated from the personal letter pastoral concern and affection. The combination was admirably suited to convey the newly recognized status and the new message. The letter itself as the *koine* form of the *koine* language in the *koine* life symbolizes and embodies this revolution, and Paul seized it for his ministry.

Paul created a letter eminently suitable for the needs of the young Gentile churches. There was a need for order and organization amid the disorder accompanying the revolution, the turning of the world upside down. The rather stereotyped patterns of the epistolary forms were models of orderliness for the life of the communities. On the other hand, indifference to the conventions regarding limitations and suitable topics allowed a disorder for meeting a variety of problems and needs as they arose. In addition, the regular protocol based on careful preparation, arrangements for delivery, and formal reception, imposed an orderliness on the letter-event. On the other hand, again, an emissary's presence and presentation gave opportunity for free exchange concerning the sender's intent and the recipients' response. Paul's freedom in adapting and transforming the available epistolary models encouraged the transformation of the people's lives while at the same time grounding them in a new kind of stability.

B. Letter Writing and Speech Writing[5]

How did Paul approach his task of communicating with the assemblies by written word? What was his mindset? Did he primarily visualize

5. See Karl P. Donfried and Johannes Beutler (eds.), *The Thessalonians Debate: Methodical Discord or Methodical Synthesis?* (Grand Rapids: Eerdmans, 2000). Although these studies were published after the major portion of this work was completed, two articles should be noted in connection with this section: Jeffrey A. D. Weima, "The Function of 1 Thessalonians 2:1-12 and the Use of Rhetorical Criticism: A Response to Otto Merk"

himself as delivering messages in speech form and in person before the people, or did he see himself as communicating the same in writing while separated from the people? Or how did he combine the two approaches?

A preliminary question asks, "why did Paul write?" An obvious answer is that he wrote because he was separated from the assemblies and unable to be present. First Thessalonians witnesses to this cause in expressing Paul's emphatic longing to revisit and through his obvious hesitancy in writing. However, between the writing of 1 Thessalonians and Romans Paul had learned to depend on letters not simply because the separation could not be conveniently bridged, but also because on occasion it proved to be a preferable means of meeting the problems and needs of the assemblies. For reconciliation with Philemon a letter of commendation must precede Paul's arrival (Phlm 21-22). In 1 Corinthians, to respond to the reports of the emissaries, he relies on his official position expressed by full sender identity, extended address, recognition of and consultation with emissaries, the *peri de* form of response to the items presented to him in writing, and his personal subscription. To this writer it seems that in this case Paul preferred to write in the officially adapted medium in order to express his authoritative decisions. The same may be said concerning the letter to Galatia. That it is intended to be presented before several assemblies would have made a trip improbable for Paul. Furthermore he would likely have been quite satisfied to meet the problems in this hostile region through written communication entrusted to emissaries. And if Romans is an open letter, a visit or visits to all possible recipients was impossible. In answer to the preliminary question, it seems that the letter was the more appropriate medium under these circumstances: recommendation of Onesimus, official responses to Corinth, and a strong word of rebuke to Galatian churches while he was advantageously separated from them. Finally, in the second letter to Corinth he gives his own reason for opting for the written word (2 Cor 2:3-4; 13:10).

Evidence that Paul saw his task of communicating as primarily one

---

(114-31; see esp. 123-31); Raymond F. Collins, "'I Command That This Letter Be Read': Writing as a Manner of Speaking" (319-39). A few references to the articles have been included above. For other studies on Pauline rhetoric consulted but not cited in this book see the listings in the Bibliography: C. C. Black; Frank Witt Hughes; George A. Kennedy; S. E. Porter and T. H. Olbricht; Wilhelm Wuellner.

of letter writing is provided by his adaptation of the official letter forms and functions. His communications were prepared, sent, and delivered according to official logistics to the extent that Paul could command them. As for the logistics, the execution of the letter-event required consultation with co-workers and emissaries, and often support by members of the congregation from which he was writing. They formed a kind of temporary chancery. Careful arrangements were made for delivery; and the letters must have been read before the assembled congregation. Note especially that the anticipation of oral presentation is as much due to the requirement of official logistics as it is to the expectation of speech writing.[6]

To this evidence of official influence may be added evidence drawn from the total setting out of which Paul wrote. The setting consists of the broad area of his ministry and the conditions that necessitated his letter writing. Paul was not a resident prophet at one location where he could deliver appropriate homilies. He was not an official with an office in a prominent city.[7] To the contrary, he was an itinerant apostle who met the responsibilities of the newly founded congregations by conceiving of his field of ministry as a network of scattered units and people. To minister to these churches when separated from them, he had to depend on the services of trusted co-workers and on the commonly accepted, omnipresent medium of letters.

The network was supported and enlivened by co-workers and emissaries reporting back and forth between the people and Paul — people whose duty it was to deliver both oral and written messages.[8] It is significant that it is often recorded that brothers accompanied the co-worker or emissary. They formed a temporary delegation of representa-

6. Concerning Demosthenes Goldstein says, after his study of the orator's rhetoric, "Hence, if the author uses the style and locutions of an oration rather than those of a letter, there is no reason to think that he forgot that he was writing and not speaking, and still less to suspect the document of inauthenticity (Jonathan A. Goldstein, *The Letters of Demosthenes* [New York: Columbia University Press, 1968], 99). Goldstein supports the genuineness of D. *Epp.* 1-4 by his rhetorical analyses. See his section, "The Rhetorical Analysis of the Letters," 133-81.

7. A longer stay was made at Galatia because of illness, and others imposed by the seasons; so he planned to spend a winter in Corinth (1 Cor 5:6). He probably used the time to write as necessary.

8. For the movement between the churches see Chap. I on delivery, 11-13.

tives and couriers. For example, Timothy returned from Corinth with the brothers and Apollos was encouraged to go to Corinth with the brothers (1 Cor 16:11-12). And a brother accompanied Titus to Corinth (2 Cor 13:18). Perhaps other congregational members unofficially attended the emissaries. A network of people was involved in the continuing communication.

Paul kept the network alive as a means for establishing and maintaining relations among the people. For this purpose he shared encouraging communications. The Corinthians were challenged to contribute to the Relief Fund by the example of the Galatians (1 Cor 16:1) and the Macedonians (2 Cor 8:1-7; 1 Thess 1:6-8). For the same purpose greetings were passed back and forth and Paul requested prayers on his behalf (1 Thess 5:25; 1 Cor 1:11). Furthermore, the network is one of continued dialogue. The exchanges are specific, ad hoc, continuous. For this kind of exchange letter writing of all types and at all times is beneficial.[9]

Finally, it may be noted here that Paul called his communications letters, and he does not request that they be disseminated beyond the people named in the salutation or be preserved.[10] The evidences of his method of composition gathered in Chapter I do not indicate an attempt on his part to write in a literary fashion or an expectation regarding his words' preservation. To the contrary, regardless of the setting, type, or intention of a letter there is something of the transient and impermanent about it. The letter is expendable. There is a direct correlation between

9. Reported misunderstandings must be corrected (1 Cor 5:9-13; 2 Cor 1:15-22), and replies are made to oral and written reports (1 Thess, 1 and 2 Cor, Phil). Cf. the give and take in the papyrus letters (White, *Light, passim*). In Welles, *Royal Cor.*, no. 7, King Lysimachus to Samos, the king offers an explanation for a previous misunderstanding concerning a decision over a land dispute; no. 15 corrects a false impression of the recipient that the writer had made in an earlier letter; no. 30 confirms an order that had previously been given in person concerning the billeting in the city of Soli. See *passim* the responses to letters received (e.g., no. 56) or to oral reports by envoys (e.g., no. 68). The writers of romances are careful to include these types of responses to simulate authenticity. See the *Letters* of Chion and the possible remnants of a romance in the *Socratic Letters*. E.g., to correct a misunderstanding, no. 1; in response to a letter received, nos. 7, 10, 11, 15, 25; and to an oral report, no. 26.

10. 1 Thess 5:27; 1 Cor 5:9; 2 Cor 7:8, 10:9-11 (collected by Collins, note 29, p. 329). See 329ff. in Raymond F. Collins, "'I Command That This Letter Be Read': Writing as a Manner of Speaking" (above, note 5). Collins argues for a synthetic analysis of 1 Thess, a combination of rhetorical composition and epistolary communication.

the sense of urgency of mission, the impermanent nature of life in expectation of the eschaton, and the ephemeral nature of a letter.

The Gentile congregations were divided and scattered and did not have a common identity. So Paul created a literature in the form of letters, and these letters by multiple addresses, intercongregational greetings, circular distribution, and use for cooperative efforts such as the Famine Relief Fund, were a means for binding together the scattered communities in a sense of common life and purpose. It is therefore strongly indicated that Paul thought in terms of letter writing and that the letter in form and function is the basic medium of Paul's communications; an observation already indicated by the salutation, thanksgiving, dual structure of background and message, and sub-epistolary forms in salutation and other entries.

In summary, the letter is the medium for the communication of reports, requests, and messages; for responses and answers, conducted often in a continued dialogical exchange. It is the official medium for the expression of the writer's authority and the transmission of the sense of his or her personal presence.[11] By the adaptation of official form and function Paul's letters are expressions of his self-identification as an intermediary between the Christ and the assemblies. The letter writer is well acquainted with delays, and conscious of the letter's reanimation, upon reception, in another's voice. He knows that he can depend on the carrier to interpret passages and to deliver oral messages. He may, therefore, write freely and not intend revision or rewriting.

On this basis the units of the communication separately and in combination with others are open for rhetorical analysis, for identification of, and clarification by, rhetorical forms and devices. Paul was a proclaimer of the gospel and an instructor in the Christian life. He naturally used persuasive and argumentative language in communications designed to meet numerous, varied, and complicated situations. However, his use of "the locutions of an orator" is enclosed in epistolary forms, functions, and settings as required by the nature and context of his ministry.

---

11. Paul's sense of the projection of his personal presence is strongly expressed in the case of his judgment of the immoral man at Corinth (1 Cor 5:1-5). For more on this see Hays' reconstruction of the incident concerning the immoral man at Corinth in *First Corinthians* (Louisville: John Knox, 1997), 80-86.

The prominence and importance of letter writing to Paul is further seen in his choice of the letter of recommendation as a paradigm of his ministry.

C. The Letter of Recommendation as a Paradigm of Paul's Ministry

In the letter of reconciliation and consolation with the Corinthians (2 Cor 1-7) Paul envisions the letter of recommendation as a paradigm of his ministry. The figure subsumes the gospel, the apostolic calling, the pattern of ministry, and the full acceptance of letter writing in the conduct of that ministry. The figure is especially fitting inasmuch as recommendation of Paul and his authority has been a source of trouble in the congregation (2 Cor 5:11-12; 6:1-10; cf. 1:12).

A severe and divisive problem has arisen between Paul and the Corinthians. In order to heal the wounds and restore good relations, Paul has written a letter and dispatched Titus to Corinth. In the official manner he has sent his written word and his emissary. His efforts have been eminently successful (2 Cor 7:5-13a). The success is a full endorsement of his theology of ministry and its epistolary arm. It is in this letter (2 Cor 1-7) that Paul chooses letter writing, particularly the letter of recommendation, as the model of his ministry.

As to the occasion, Paul has in mind his previous letter to Corinth and its success in restoring good relationships. He reviews the occasion and the purpose for that writing,

> And I wrote you as I did, so that when I came, I might not suffer pain from those who should have made me rejoice; for I am confident about all of you, that my joy would be the joy of all of you. For I wrote you out of much distress and anguish of heart and with many tears, not to cause you pain, but to let you know the abundant love I have for you. (2 Cor 2:3-4; cf. 7:8, 12)

The successful ministry elicits a paean of consolation (1:3-7). Thereupon Paul seeks a fitting figure to symbolize this exemplary experience. He tries the triumphal procession and the fragrance of incense (2:14-16). But they do not accommodate the word or the Presence, and he does not develop them. A contrast with peddlers offers the elements of ministry missing in the two previous figures,

> For we are not peddlers of God's word like so many; but in Christ we speak as persons of sincerity, as persons sent from God and standing in his presence. (2:17)

At once the problem of self-recommendation, solved by reconciliation through the media of letter and emissary, brings to mind the analogy that Paul first develops: the letter of recommendation embodies the essence of his ministry. Such an image, after his Corinthian experience, comes readily to Paul's mind, especially in view of the criticism about his self-recommendation. The logistics and setting of a letter of recommendation and its components reveal the central and primary significance of this figure. Paul was well acquainted with and made use of this type of letter. He recommends Phoebe to the Roman congregation (Rom 16:1); Onesimus to Philemon and the house church. Philemon in itself as a letter of commendation incorporates this metaphor for Paul's ministry.[12] Paul commends Titus and the other members of the Famine Relief Fund to the Corinthians (2 Cor. 8:16-24). There is an apologetic self-recommendation in the catalogue of hardships included in a letter from an earlier date (2 Cor. 11:16-33). This self-recommendation is repeated in the lesser catalogue in this letter (6:3-10; see 5:12). His lack of documented recommendation is aggravated by those who ask for or actually hold, "as some do, letters of recommendation to you or from you" (3:1). Perhaps Paul recalls the letters which he carried to authorize his persecution of Christians.[13]

The verses, 2 Corinthians 3:1-3, are here translated,

---

12. See Chap. III, "The Letters." Hooker calls the letter of recommendation a "brilliant metaphor" for Paul's ministry (Morna Hooker, "Beyond the Things That Are Written? St. Paul's Use of Scripture," *NTS* 27 [1981], 296). This most appropriate metaphor was called to my attention by Scott J. Hafemann, *Suffering and Ministry in the Spirit: Paul's Defense of His Ministry in II Corinthians 2:14–3:3* (Grand Rapids: Eerdmans, 1990), 189. For the extent to which Paul had in mind the letter of recommendation when writing the Corinthian correspondence see Victor Paul Furnish, *II Corinthians,* Anchor Bible (Garden City, NY: Doubleday, 1984), 192-96.

13. See also later letters of recommendation or transfer, Chan-Hie Kim, *Form and Structure of the Familiar Greek Letter of Recommendation,* SBLDS 4 (1972), nos. 76-78.

Are we, I and Titus and the others, beginning again to commend ourselves?[14] Or do we need as some do letters of recommendation to you or from you? You are our letter of recommendation, written on our hearts (that is, ours and yours), known and read by all people. You show[15] that you are a letter of Christ serviced by us: recorded, delivered, and publicly presented;[16] written not with ink but with the Spirit of the living God; not on tablets of stone but on tablets of human hearts. (author's translation)

The author, composer, is Christ. He is the one who originates the message and provides the authority. He knows the one to be recommended.

The message, the recommendation, is the Corinthian congregation itself, "You yourselves are our letter." Its theme is one of reconciliation. Out of this experience Paul finds reconciliation as the summary of the gospel: God's act in Christ Jesus, and the continuing work of the Spirit (5:17-21). This good news is actualized in and by the congregation

14. I interpret the first person plural, "our hearts," in 3:1 to indicate that Paul is sharing the ministry and its joyous outcome with his co-workers, namely Silvanus and Timothy (1:19) and Titus (2:13; 7:6; 8:23). In verse 2, "you are our letter" refers to the Corinthians and "written on our hearts" is, therefore, inclusive, i.e. "yours and ours" (see margin). For the sharing of authority with Timothy in Philippians see Franz Schnider and Werner Stenger, *Studien zum neutestamentlichen Briefformular* (Leiden: Brill, 1987), 4.

15. Paul refers to the reputation of his churches; note the generalized addresses on 1 Cor 1:2 and 2 Cor 1:1; cf. Rom 1:8; and the reputation of the Corinthians for which Paul gives thanks, 1 Cor 1:4-9. In like manner the Thessalonians will be Paul's boast at the Lord's coming, 1 Thess 2:19-20. Regarding 2 Cor 3:2-5 Crafton writes, "In a show of rhetorical brilliance Paul engages the Corinthians in his argument by naming *them* as the sign of his agency. *They* are proof of his apostolic effectiveness, of his authenticity" (Jeffrey A. Crafton, *The Agency of the Apostle: A Dramatistic Analysis of Paul's Responses to Conflict in 2 Corinthians*, JSNT Sup 51 [Sheffield: JSOT Press, 1991], 80, Crafton's emphasis). Crafton *(ibid.)* quotes C. K. Barrett *(A Commentary on the Second Epistle to the Corinthians*, 108), "The existence of the Corinthian Christians in Christ is a communication of Christ to the world."

16. *diakonētheisa*, servicing a letter, embraces the whole logistics: recording, delivery, and public presentation. Cf. Paul's use of the term in reference to the Famine Relief Fund, 2 Cor 8:19-20; the Fund was serviced: collected, delivered, and presented by the commissioners. *BAG* refers to J. *Ant.* 6 298, "for a service consisting of a message," s.v. *diakoneō*, 2; and to this passage, "A letter of Christ cared for (i.e. written or delivered)," *ibid.*, 3. The metaphor requires the fulfilment of the logistics, the public reading, i.e. the gospel is proclaimed by the very existence of the congregation.

through Paul's ministry as an apostle. The message is the very existence
of the Corinthian congregation and its exemplary response (cf. 2 Cor
1:12-14).

The writing materials are human hearts, not stone; the Spirit, not
ink (3:3). The parchment is the hearts of Paul, his helpers, and the heart
of the incorporated believers. "You are our letter, written on [all] our
hearts. . . ." The human agency for recording and proclaiming the good
news is the whole community: ministers and people.

The amanuenses are Paul and his co-workers. Paul shares this office
with his helpers. They all are authorized by God in Christ; they are persons sent from God and standing in his presence (2:17; cf. 3:4-6).

In the pouring out of this metaphor the functions become merged.
The people are the message, a public message, but they also serve as
carriers and proclaimers. The ministers are in turn part of the parchment, amanuenses, carriers. But the central theme of the metaphor
centers on Paul as the carrier, the one recommended. As was the custom with such letters, the one recommended delivered the letter, and in
this situation Paul is the one recommended by Christ. Thus Paul is the
official carrier, an apostle (1:1), ambassador (5:20), commissioned (1:21);
the minister of a new covenant (3:6). Personal delivery assured immediate introduction of the carrier to the recipients. The one recommended
presents himself to all those who hear the public reading of the letter.

On reception the open letter of recommendation is broadcasted. It
is not just written on parchment and publicly read; it is not to be inscribed on stone. It cannot be so limited. Rather, the message of reconciliation and commendation, written "with the Spirit of the living
God" and written on the human hearts, is "to be known and read by
all." The message is unconfined, irrepressible. Such recommendation is
far greater than any human document Paul might carry.[17]

Finally, the fact that God's letter is not engraved on stone, like the
imperial, official letters of his day, reminds Paul of the stone tablets of
the old covenant and gives him a shift in the metaphor for contrasting

---

17. Letters of recommendation were publicly read when community endorsement of
the recommendation was desired as in the case of Onesimus; when envoys were presented to a community (2 Cor 8-9; Acts 15:22-29); or to relate two communities through
the one recommended and through the greetings which that one delivered (Rom 16).
For public reading see Chap. I, "The Logistics of Ancient Greek Letter-Writing."

the fading beauty of the old against the permanent glory of the new (3:7-11).[18]

In this letter (2 Cor. 1-7), then, Paul composes a paean of consolation (1:3-7) and rejoices over reconciliation with the Corinthians. He reviews their strained relationship and its healing (1:3–2:13). At the crucial point of his writing, at the heart of this joyous letter, he finds an image capable of expressing the very essence of his ministry — both its theological basis and its present material agency: the letter. That Paul relies on such a metaphor reveals the high regard he has gained for letter writing and the integral part it plays in his ministry.

18. See Hays' exegesis of this metaphor, Richard B. Hays, *Echoes of Scripture in the Letters of Paul* (New Haven: Yale Univ. Press, 1989), 131-40; Carol Kern Stockhausen, *Moses' Veil and the Glory of the New Covenant: The Exegetical Substructure of II Cor. 3,1–4,6,* Analecta Biblica 116 (Rome: Pontificio Instituto Biblico, 1989); see esp. Chapter One, "II Corinthians 3:1-6," pp. 33-86; Linda L. Belleville, *Reflections of Glory: Paul's Polemical Use of the Moses-Doxa Tradition in 2 Corinthians 3:1-18,* JSNT Sup 52 (Sheffield: JSOT Press, 1991). For the figures of procession, aroma, and letter of recommendation see Scott J. Hafemann, *Suffering and Ministry in the Spirit* (above, note 12), 37-45 and 186-225.

Appendix

(Line numbering approximates that of the Greek text)

1. Welles, no. 14 (262-261 BCE)

Salutation:

King Ptolemy to the council and people of Miletus, greeting.

Body:

The background past:

I have in former times *[kai proteron]* shown all zeal on behalf of your city both through a gift of land and through care in all other matters as was proper because I saw that our father was kindly disposed toward the city and was the author of many benefits for you and relieved you of harsh and oppressive taxes and tolls which certain of the kings had imposed.

The background present:

Now also *[nyni te]*, as you guard steadfastly your city and our friendship *[philia]* and alliance — for my son and Callicrates and the other friends who are with you have written me what a demonstration you have made of good-will toward us —

The message, commendation, promise, request:

knowing these things we praise you highly, and shall try to re-
quite your people through benefactions, and we summon you
for the future to maintain the same policy of friendship toward
us so that in view of your faithfulness we may exercise even more
our care for the city.

Concluding instruction to the envoy:

We have ordered Hegestratus to address you at greater length on
these subjects and to give you our greeting.

Farewell.

2. Welles, no. 15

King Antiochus to the council and people of Erythrae, greeting.

Background, minuted review of meeting with envoys:

Tharsynon and Pythes and Bottas, your envoys, delivered to us
the decree by which you voted our honors, and the wreath with
which you 5) crowned us, and gave us likewise the gold intended
as a present. Having discoursed on the good-will which you have
always felt toward our house and on the gratitude which your
people entertain toward all its benefactors generally, and likewise
on the esteem which your city enjoyed under the 10) former
kings, they asked with all earnestness and zeal that we should be
friendly [*philkōs*] to you and should aid in advancing the city's interest in all that refers to glory and honor. We have then accepted
in a friendly spirit the honors and the wreath and the present
also, and we praise you for 15) being grateful in all things 15) — for
you seem generally to pursue this as your policy. We have therefore from the beginning entertained good-will [*eunoian*] toward
you, seeing that you act sincerely and honestly in all matters, and
we are now even more attracted to you, recognizing your nobility
from many other things and to no small extent 20) from the decree which has been delivered to us and from the words of the envoys.

Reason for decision:

> Since Tharsynon and Pythes and Bottas have shown that under Alexander and Antigonus your city was autonomous and tax-free, while our ancestors were always zealous on its behalf; since 25) we see that their policy was just and since we ourselves wish not to lag behind in confirming favors,

Decision:

> we shall help you to maintain your autonomy and we grant you exemption not only from other taxes but even from contributions to the Gallic fund.

Promise a request for reciprocal response:

> 30) You shall have also [. . . and] any other benefit which we may think of or [you ask for]. We summon you also remembering that [we have always] tried earnestly . . . good-will as is just and . . . consistent with your previous actions . . . that you will remember suitably those [by whom] you have been benefitted.

Closing commendation of envoys:

> 35) [More about these matters and] the other questions which we discussed [will be reported to you by your] envoys, whom [we praise for their conduct] in general and especially for the concern they have shown [for the interests of your people].

Farewell.

3. Welles, no. 32

King Antiochus to the council and people of Magnesia, greeting.

Background and minuting the envoys' report:

> Demophon and Philiscus and Pheres, the envoys sent by you to my father 5) to proclaim the games and the other honors which your people have voted to perform every four years for the mistress of the city Artemis Leucophryene, 10) delivered the decree addressed to me also and spoke with enthusiasm in accordance with its contents,

The request:

> summoning me to recognize as "crowned" and of Pythian rank the games which you hold in honor of the goddess.

Reason for complying with the request:

> 15) Since my father has the kindliest feelings toward your people and has given his approval in this case, being anxious myself to follow his policy,

Request granted:

> 20) I approve the honors voted the goddess by you now

Promise:

> and in the future shall try following my father's example to aid you in furthering them in whatever matters you summon me or I myself think of.

Farewell.

4. Welles, no. 58 (between 163-156 BCE)

"[The letter] is nothing but a form . . . a collection of chancery phrases." (p. 259)

Salutation:

Attalus to priest Attis, greeting.

Health wish:

> If you were well it would be well; I also was in good health.

Body (Background, acknowledgment of envoys and review of their report):

> Menodorus, whom you sent to me, gave me your letter, assiduous and friendly as it was, and spoke at considerable length on the matters on which he said he had instructions.

Message, approval and grounds thereof:

> I have, accordingly approved your policy because I have seen you on every occasion enthusiastic in our interest,

Concluding instruction to envoy:

> and having communicated to him what I thought you ought to know I have told him to report to you.

Farewell.

5. Sherk, no. 34 = Viereck, no. II

Salutation:

> Marcus Valerius, son of Marcus, strategus, [the] tribunes and the senate to the council and people of Teos greeting.

Body:

> The background (recognition of the envoy and confirmation of the oral and written communication):
>
> Menippus who was sent to us as envoy from King Antiochus and who was appointed by you to serve as envoy on behalf of the city, delivered the decree, and he himself spoke with all zeal in accordance with it.

Basis for decision:

> We received him favorably and heard him as a friend *[philos]* because of the good repute he presented and because of the genuine courtesy toward the matters about which he inquired. We also heard him as a friend because we continually express our piety toward the gods as any one may readily infer from the goodwill we experience at the hand of the divine in these relationships. Furthermore we are persuaded from many other sources that your high honor to the divinity is evident to all.

Decision:

> Therefore, because of these considerations, your goodwill toward us, and your worthy envoy, we render judgment that the city and country are sacred, just as they now are, and also inviolate and freed from tribute by the Roman people,

Promise:

> and we shall try to increase both honors to the god and benefactions to you provided you observe henceforth your goodwill toward us.

Farewell.

6. Sherk, no. 35

Lucius Cornelius Scipio, Consul of the Romans, and Publius Scipio, brother, to the Council and People of the Heracleans' greeting.

Background:

> 5) The envoys from you have appeared before us [seven names legible], honorable men, who presented the decree and themselves spoke in support of the matters set forth in the decree omitting nothing worthy of special notice.

Basis for decision:

> We are favorably disposed to all Greeks, and, since you have joined us in our [your] pledge,* we shall try to give all possible consideration, being always the source of some good.

Decision:

> 10) We concede to you your freedom just as [we do] to the other cities, as many as have given us protectorate over them; [we concede also to you] the right to govern all your affairs according to your laws;

Promise:

> and in other respects we, being favorable to you, shall try always to be the source of some good. 15) We accept the kindnesses [gifts] from you and the pledges, and we ourselves shall try in no way to be surpassed in returning favors.

Closing:

> We have sent to you Lucius Orbius to have concern for your city

and country that no one annoy you. Farewell. — (author's translation)

Note: *paragegonotōn hymōn eis tēn hemeteram pistim* (line 8). The participle, "since you have joined us," i.e. "come to our support," "come to our side," suggests that some sense of the personal presence of the Heracleans has been conveyed. Furthermore, emending *hemeteram* to *hymeteram* ("since you have joined us in *your* pledge,") makes better sense and adds to the sense of the Heracleans' presence. See lines 5 and 15.

7. Sherk, no. 57

Marcus Antonius, saluted imperator, one of the triumvirs for re-establishing the Republic, to the Assembly of the Greeks in Asia, greeting.

Background, past (minute of previous agreement):

Even before this [*kai proteron*], when my friend and trainer Marcus Antonius Artemidorus met me at Ephesus with Charopinus of Ephesus, eponymous priest of the guild of world champions and crowned victors at the sacred games, with the petition that the existing privileges of the guild should remain unimpaired and that it might be granted to write forthwith to you in regard to the other grants and privileges that were requested from me, namely, freedom from military service, complete immunity from public duties, exemption from billeting, truce at the time of assembly, inviolability of members, and the right to wear purple,

Reason for previous agreement:

I willingly granted these, both because of my friend Artemidorus and because of my desire to do a favor to their eponymous priest, not only for the honor but also for the enhancement of the guild.

Background, present:

So also now [*kai ta nyn*], when Artemidorus came to me again with the request that they should be permitted to erect a bronze tablet and to engrave upon it the grant of the above-mentioned privileges,

Reason for present decision:

I desired to fail Artemidorus in no way in respect to his mission

Decision:

and I grant the right to have the tablet, as he requests.

Subscript:

I am confirming this in a letter to you. (Johnson, *Statutes,* no. 125)

8. Josephus, *Life* 216-18

Jonathan and his fellow deputies [*hoi syn autōi*, i.e., the deputies with him] from Jerusalem to Josephus, greeting.

Background:

The Jerusalem authorities, having heard that John of Gischala has frequently plotted against you, have commissioned us to reprove him and to admonish him in the future to show you proper respect.

Reason for request:

Wishing to confer with you on a concerted line of action,

The request:

we request you to come to us with all speed, and with but few attendants, as this village could not accommodate a large military force. (Thackeray)

9. Josephus, *Life* 226-27

Josephus to Jonathan and his colleagues [*tois syn autōi*, i.e., the deputies with him], greeting.

Background, acknowledgment of communication [letter?] received:

> I am delighted to hear that you have reached Galilee in good health; more especially because I shall now be able to hand over to you the charge of affairs here and return home, as I have long wished to do.

Present situation and reason for following request:

> I ought certainly to have gone, not merely to Xaloth, but further, to wait upon you, even without your instructions; I must, however, request you to excuse me for my inability to do so, as I am here at Chabolo, keeping watch on Placidus, who is meditating an incursion up country into Galilee.

Request:

> Do you, therefore, on receipt of this letter, come and visit me.

Fare you well. (Thackeray)

10. Josephus, *JA.* 13 127-28

Heading:

> King Demetrius to his father Lasthenes, greeting.

Background:

> The Jewish nation is friendly to us.

Decision:

> I have decided to give three districts to it.

Order:

> See to it, therefore, that a copy of these instructions be made and set up in a conspicuous place in the holy temple.

Farewell.

11. White, *Petition*, no. 14

To Asclepiades, king's cousin and strategus,

Sender identification:

> from Dionysius son of Cephalas, cultivator of Crown land, of the village of Tenis also called Akoris in the Mochite district.

Background:

> For reasons which will be indicated in the course of the affair I and my mother Senabollous made with Admetus also called Chesthotes, of the same village, a contract of loan through the record-office for 150 artabae of wheat in the 9th year; not only so, but I also made with him for guarantee a contract of mortgage on the unoccupied sites which I possess.

Reason for request:

> Having obtained these agreements the accused performed none of the things about which we had come to terms, whereby he has caused me no slight damage; and now on wrongful grounds, seeing me busily engaged in sowing the land which I cultivate, he persecutes me and does not allow me to attend to the cultivation in spite of the decrees repeatedly issued about us cultivators; wherefore as the land threatens to get out of hand, being unable at present to go to law with him about the agreements, I have been compelled to seek your protection.

Request:

> I request you, if you approve, to give orders first of all for a letter to be written to the epistates of Akoris not to allow the accused to molest either me or my mother, and to give me a safe-conduct in writing, until I have finished the sowing and can settle accounts with him on every point.

Additional reason for request:

> By this means none of the king's interests will suffer, while I myself shall obtain relief.

Farewell.

12. White, *Petition*, no. 23

Heading:

To Dionysodorus, strategus of the Arsinoite nome, from Mysthes and Pelopion both sons of Pelops, of Euhemeris in the division of Themistes.

Body, background:

[Date] as I was making an inspection of the lands which we farm belonging to Marcus Apollonius Saturnius in the area of the aforesaid village, we found that the young wheat and the barley which we have on the farm had been grazed down by the sheep of Harmiusis son of Heras, herdsman, Aunes son of Minches, being witness to it; the consequent damage amounts to five artabae of wheat and nine artabae of barley.

Request:

I therefore request that he be brought before you for the ensuing punishment.

Farewell.

13. White, *Light*, no. 30

Sender identification:

Eirene, daughter of Orphis, a Macedonian woman, with her guardian, her husband, Agamemnon, son of Chrysermos, a native of Lalassis, to Leontiskos, Thymos and Tesenouphis.

The message:

I agree with you that you are to pay off to Nikandros, Syracusan, the rent of the entire orchard, forty-eight talents of copper, in the time specified according to the lease and, [assuming] you perform the terms of the agreement, that I am not to indict you concerning these matters. Good-bye. (Year) 23, Tybi 29.

Subscription of confirmation [second hand]:

I agree to the above-written statements.

14. *POxy* 2108 (259 CE)

Heading:

> Aurelius Serapion also called . . . rion, strategus of the Hermopolite nome, to his most dear Aurelii, Diodorus also called Dionys . . . , ex-eutheniarch of Alexandria, and Demetrius also called Numenius, ex-eutheniarch of Alexandria, eirenarchs of Mochite and Pasko, greeting.

Background:

> Their excellencies the senate have forwarded to me an announcement to be displayed in the most conspicuous places in the villages.

Request (polite order):

> I accordingly send you a copy, dear friends, in order that you may cause it to be displayed in every village.

Closing (second hand):

> I pray for your health.

15. Demosthenes, *Or.* 18 *(De Corona)* 39

> Philip, King of Macedonia, to the Council and People of Athens, greeting.

Background, the past:

> Know that we have passed within the Gates, and have subdued the district of Phocis. We have put garrisons in all the fortified places that surrendered voluntarily; those that did not obey we have stormed and razed to the ground, selling the inhabitants into slavery.

The present:

> Hearing that you are actually preparing an expedition to help them, I have written to you to save you further trouble in this matter.

Grounds for the warning:

> Your general policy strikes me as unreasonable, to agree to peace, and yet take the field against me, and that although the Phocians were not included in the terms on which we agreed.

The message, a warning:

> Therefore if you decline to abide by your agreements, you will gain no advantage save that of being the aggressors. (Vince)

16. White, *Light,* no. 88, Claudius to Alexandria

After the salutation and greetings (ll. 1-16) are two extended sections. They form the response to the envoy's oral presentation. In the first (ll. 16-28) Claudius names and gives special recognition to the envoys. In the second (ll. 29-51) he accepts the honors and gives detailed instructions concerning their disposition. There follows the items introduced by peri de *(ll. 52-78), marking them as responses to the written communication.*

52 Concerning the requests which you have been anxious to receive from me, I decide as follows.

62 Concerning [your suggestion that] the municipal magistrates be triennial, it seems to me you have decided well . . . .

66 Regarding *[peri de]* the senate, what indeed your custom was under ancient kings, I have no way of saying . . . .

72 As to who should be held responsible for the disorder and sedition against the Jews [genitive case without *peri de*] . . . .

Bibliography

Achtemeier, Paul J. "*Omne Verbum Sonat:* The New Testament and the Oral Environment of Late Western Antiquity." *Journal of Biblical Literature* 109 (1990): 3-27.

Agnew, Francis H. "The Origin of the NT Apostle-Concept: A Review of Research." *Journal of Biblical Literature* 105 (1986): 75-96.

Alexander, Loveday. "Hellenistic Letter-Forms and the Structure of Philippians." *Journal for the Study of the New Testament* 37 (1989): 87-101.

Alexander, P. S. "Epistolary Literature." Pages 579-96 in *Jewish Writings of the Second Temple Period.* Edited by Michael E. Stone. Assen: Van Gorcum; Philadelphia: Fortress, 1984.

Alter, Robert, and Frank Kermode, eds. *The Literary Guide to the Bible.* Cambridge, MA: Belknap Press, 1987.

Andresen, Carl. "Zum Formular Früchristlicher Gemeindebriefe." *Zeitschrift für die neutestamentliche Wissenschaft und die Kunde der älteren Kirche* 56 (1965): 233-59.

Auerbach, Eric. *Mimesis: The Representation of Reality in Western Literature.* Princeton: Princeton University Press, 1953.

Aune, David E., ed. *Greco-Roman Literature and the New Testament: Selected Forms and Genres.* Society of Biblical Literature Sources for Biblical Study 21. Atlanta: Scholars Press, 1988.

———. *The New Testament in Its Literary Environment.* Library of Early Christianity 8. Philadelphia: Westminster Press, 1987.

Bahr, Gordon J. "Paul and Letter Writing in the First Century." *Catholic Biblical Quarterly* 28 (1966): 465-77.

———. "The Subscriptions in the Pauline Letters." *Journal of Biblical Literature* 87 (1968): 27-41.

Bailey, James L., and Lyle D. Vander Broek. *Literary Forms in the New Testament: A Handbook.* Louisville: Westminster/John Knox, 1992.

Baird, William. *The Corinthian Church — A Biblical Approach to Urban Culture.* Nashville: Abingdon, 1964.

Balch, David L., Everett Ferguson, and Wayne A. Meeks, eds. *Greeks, Romans, and Christians: Essays in Honor of Abraham J. Malherbe.* Minneapolis: Fortress, 1990.

Banks, Robert J. *Paul's Idea of Community: The Early House Churches in Their Cultural Setting.* Revised and updated edition. Peabody, MA: Hendrickson, 1994.

Barrett, C. K. *A Commentary on the First Epistle to the Corinthians.* New York: Harper and Row, 1968.

———. *A Commentary on the Second Epistle to the Corinthians.* New York: Harper and Row, 1973.

Bartlett, David L. *Ministry in the New Testament.* Overtures to Biblical Theology. Minneapolis: Fortress, 1993.

Bassler, Jouette M., ed. *Pauline Theology Volume I: Thessalonians, Philippians, Galatians, Philemon.* Minneapolis: Fortress, 1991.

Beardslee, William A. *Literary Criticism of the New Testament.* Philadelphia: Fortress, 1970.

Becker, Jürgen. *Paul: Apostle to the Gentiles.* Louisville: Westminster/John Knox, 1993.

Belleville, Linda L. *Reflections of Glory: Paul's Polemical Use of the Moses-Doxa Tradition in 2 Corinthians 3:1-18.* Journal for the Study of the New Testament Supplement Series 52. Sheffield: JSOT Press, 1991.

———. "Continuity or Discontinuity: A Fresh Look at 1 Corinthians in the Light of First-Century Epistolary Forms and Conventions." *Evangelical Quarterly* 59 (1987): 15-37.

Berger, Klaus. "Apostelbrief und apostolische Rede: Zum Formular Frühchristlischer Briefe." Pages 190-231 in *The Thessalonian Correspondence.* Edited by Raymond F. Collins. Leuven: Leuven University Press/Peeters, 1990.

Betz, Hans Dieter. *Galatians: A Commentary on Paul's Letter to the Churches in Galatia.* Hermeneia. Philadelphia: Fortress, 1979.

———. *2 Corinthians 8 and 9: A Commentary on Two Administrative Letters of the Apostle Paul.* Hermeneia. Philadelphia: Fortress, 1985.

Bieringer, Reimund. "Paul's Divine Jealousy: The Apostle and His Communities in Relationship." *Louvain Studies* 17 (1992): 197-231.

Binder, Hermann. "Paulus und die Thessalonischerbriefe." Pages 87-93 in *The Thessalonian Correspondence.* Edited by Raymond F. Collins. Leuven: Leuven University Press/Peeters, 1990.

Bjerkelund, Carl J. *Parakalô: Form, Function und Sinn der parakalô-Sätze in den paulinischen Briefen.* Oslo: Universitetsforlaget, 1967.

Black, C. C. "Rhetorical Questions: The New Testament, Classical Rhetoric, and Current Interpretations." *Dialog* 19 (1990): 62-70.

Botha, P. J. J. "Greco-Roman Literacy as Setting for New Testament Writings." *Neotestamentica* 26 (1992): 195-215.

Branick, Vincent P. *The House Church in the Writings of Paul.* Wilmington: Michael Glazier, 1989.

Broneer, Oscar. "Corinth, Center of Paul's Missionary Work in Greece." *Biblical Archaeologist* 14 (1951).

———. "The Isthmian Games." *Biblical Archaeologist* 25 (1962).

Church, F. Forrester. "Rhetorical Structure and Design in Paul's Letter to Philemon." *Harvard Theological Review* 17 (1968): 17-33.

Clark, W. P. "Ancient Reading." *Classical Journal* 26 (1930-31): 698-700.

Collins, Raymond F. *Studies on the First Letter to the Thessalonians.* Leuven: Leuven University Press/Peeters, 1984.

———. "'. . . that this letter be read to all the brethren.' A New Testament Note." *Louvain Studies* 9 (1982): 122-27.

Collins, Raymond F., ed. *The Thessalonian Correspondence.* Leuven: Leuven University Press/Peeters, 1990.

Conzelmann, Hans. *1 Corinthians.* Philadelphia: Fortress, 1975.

Cook, David. "The Prescript as Programme in Galatians." *Journal of Theological Studies* 43 (1992): 511-19.

Cowley, Arthur. *Aramaic Papyri of the Fifth Century B.C. Edited with Translation and Notes.* 1923. Repr., Osnabruck: O. Zeller, 1967.

Craddock, Fred B. *Philippians.* Interpretation: A Bible Commentary for Teaching and Preaching. Atlanta: John Knox, 1985.

Crafton, Jeffrey A. *The Agency of the Apostle: A Dramatistic Analysis of Paul's Responses to Conflict in 2 Corinthians.* Journal for the Study of the New Testament Supplement Series 51. Sheffield: JSOT Press, 1991.

Crönert, W. "Die beiden ältesten griechischen Briefe." *Rein Mus* 65 (1910): 157-60.

Crossan, John Dominic. *Jesus: A Revolutionary Biography.* San Francisco: HarperSanFrancisco, 1994.

Cullmann, Oscar. *Early Christian Worship.* Studies in Biblical Theology 10. London: SCM Press, 1953.

Dahl, Nils A. "Paul and the Church at Corinth according to I Corinthians 1-4." Pages 313-35 in *Christian History and Interpretation: Studies Presented to John Knox.* Edited by W. R. Farmer, C. F. D. Moule, and R. R. Niebuhr. Cambridge: Cambridge University Press, 1967. Repr., pages 40-61 in *Studies in Paul: Theology for the Early Christian Mission.* Minneapolis: Augsburg, 1977.

————. "Letters." Pages 538-40 in *The Interpreter's Dictionary of the Bible: Supplementary Volume.* Edited by K. Crim. Nashville: Abingdon, 1976.

Deissmann, Gustav Adolf. *Bible Studies.* Edinburgh, 1901.

————. *Light from the Ancient East.* London, 1927.

————. *St. Paul.* New York and London, 1912.

————. *The New Testament in the Light of Modern Research.* The Haskell Lectures. New York, 1929.

Demming, Will. "The Unity of 1 Corinthians 5-6." *Journal of Biblical Literature* 115 (1996): 289-312.

Dix, Gregory. *Jew and Greek: A Study in the Primitive Church.* Westminster: Dacre Press, 1953.

Dockery, David S. "The Shape of Life in the Spirit in Pauline Thought." Pages 49-76 in *Scribes and Scripture: New Testament Essays in Honor of J. Harold Greenlee.* Edited by David Alan Black. Winona Lake, IN: Eisenbrauns, 1992.

Donfried, Karl P. "The Theology of One Thessalonians as a Reflection of Its Purpose." Pages 243-60 in *To Touch the Text: Biblical and Related Studies in Honor of Joseph A. Fitzmyer, S.J.* Edited by Maurya P. Horgan and Paul J. Kobelski. New York: Crossroad Publishing Co., 1989.

————. "1 Thessalonians, Acts, and the Early Paul." Pages 3-26 in *The Thessalonian Correspondence.* Edited by Raymond F. Collins. Leuven: Leuven University Press/Peeters, 1990.

Donfried, Karl P., ed. *The Romans Debate.* Revised and expanded edition. Peabody, MA: Hendrickson, 1991.

Donfried, Karl P., and Johannes Beutler, eds. *The Thessalonians Debate: Methodical Discord or Methodical Synthesis?* Grand Rapids: Eerdmans, 2000.

Dorsey, C. "Paul's Use of Apostolos." *Restoration Quarterly* 28 (1985-86): 193-200.

Doty, William G. "The Classification of Epistolary Literature." *Catholic Biblical Quarterly* 31 (1969): 183-99.

————. *Letters in Primitive Christianity.* Philadelphia: Fortress, 1973.

Driver, G. R. *Aramaic Documents of the Fifth Century B.C.* Abridged revised edition. Oxford: Clarendon Press, 1954.

Drury, John. "Mark." Pages 402-17 in *The Literary Guide to the Bible.* Edited by Robert Alter and Frank Kermode. Cambridge, MA: Belknap Press, 1987.

Dunn, J. D. G. "2 Corinthians III,17 'The Lord is the Spirit.'" *Journal of Theological Studies* 21 (1970): 309-20.

Ellis, E. Earle. "Paul and His Co-Workers." *New Testament Studies* 17 (1970-71): 435-52.

Epp, Eldon Jay. "New Testament Papyrus Manuscripts and Letter Carrying in Greco-Roman Times." Pages 35-56 in *The Future of Early Christianity: Essays in Honor of Helmut Koester.* Edited by Birger A. Pearson. Minneapolis: Fortress, 1991.

Exler, Francis X. J. *The Form of the Ancient Greek Letter: A Study in Greek Epistolography.* Washington, DC: Catholic University of America, 1923.

Farmer, W. R., C. F. D. Moule, and R. R. Niebuhr, eds. *Christian History and Interpretation: Studies Presented to John Knox.* Cambridge, MA: Cambridge University Press, 1967.

Fee, Gordon D. *God's Empowering Presence: The Holy Spirit in the Letters of Paul.* Peabody, MA: Hendrickson, 1994.

———. "Toward a Theology of 1 Corinthians." Pages 37-58 in *Pauline Theology Volume II: 1 and 2 Corinthians.* Edited by David M. Hay. Minneapolis: Fortress, 1993.

Fitzgerald, John T., ed. *Friendship, Flattery, and Frankness of Speech: Studies on Friendship in the New Testament World.* Novum Testamentum Supplements 82. Leiden: E. J. Brill, 1996.

———. *Greco-Roman Perspectives on Friendship.* Society of Biblical Literature Sources for Biblical Study. Atlanta: Scholars Press, 1996.

Fitzgerald, John T. "Paul, the Ancient Epistolary Theorists, and 2 Corinthians 10–13." Pages 190-200 in *Greeks, Romans, and Christians: Essays in Honor of Abraham J. Malherbe.* Edited by David L. Balch, Everett Ferguson, and Wayne A. Meeks. Minneapolis: Fortress, 1990.

Fitzmyer, Joseph A. *According to Paul: Studies in the Theology of the Apostle.* New York: Paulist Press, 1993.

———. *Romans: A New Translation with Introduction and Commentary.* The Anchor Bible. New York: Doubleday, 1993.

———. *The Letter to Philemon: A New Translation with Introduction and Commentary.* The Anchor Bible. New York: Doubleday, 2000.

Foerster, Werner. "Abfassungszeit und Ziel des Galaterbriefes." Pages 135-41 in *Apophoreta: Festschrift für Ernst Haenchen.* Edited by W. Eltester and F. H. Kettler. Berlin: Töpelmann, 1964.

Fortna, Robert T., and Beverly R. Gaventa, eds. *The Conversation Continues: Studies in Paul and John in Honor of J. Louis Martyn.* Nashville: Abingdon, 1990.

Funk, Robert W. *Language, Hermeneutic, and Word of God: The Problem of Language in the New Testament and Contemporary Theology.* New York: Harper and Row, 1966.

———. "The Apostolic *Parousia*: Form and Significance." Pages 249-86 in *Christian History and Interpretation: Studies Presented to John Knox.* Edited by W. R. Farmer, C. F. D. Moule, and R. R. Niebuhr. Cambridge: Cambridge University Press, 1967.

Furnish, Victor Paul. *II Corinthians: A New Translation with Introduction and Commentary.* The Anchor Bible. Garden City, NY: Doubleday, 1984.

————. "Theology in 1 Corinthians." Pages 69-74 in *Pauline Theology Volume II: 1 and 2 Corinthians.* Edited by David M. Hay. Minneapolis: Fortress, 1993.

Gamble, Harry Jr. *The Textual History of the Letter to the Romans: A Study in Textual and Literary Criticism.* Studies and Documents 42. Grand Rapids: Eerdmans, 1977.

Gaventa, Beverly Roberts. "The Singularity of the Gospel: A Reading of Galatians." Pages 147-59 in *Pauline Theology Volume I: Thessalonians, Philippians, Galatians, Philemon.* Edited by Jouette M. Bassler. Minneapolis: Fortress, 1991.

Georgi, Dieter. *Remembering the Poor: The History of Paul's Collection for Jerusalem.* Nashville: Abingdon, 1992.

Getty, Mary Ann. "The Imitation of Paul in the Letters to the Thessalonians." Pages 277-83 in *The Thessalonian Correspondence.* Edited by Raymond F. Collins. Leuven: Leuven University Press/Peeters, 1990.

Gilchrist, J. M. "Paul and the Corinthians — The Sequence of Letters and Visits." *Journal for the Study of the New Testament* 34 (1988): 47-69.

Gilliard, Frank D. "More Silent Reading in Antiquity: *Non Omne Verbum Sonabat.*" *Journal of Biblical Literature* 112 (1993): 689-94.

Gillman, J. "Paul's *EISODOS:* The Proclaimed and the Proclaimer (1 Thess 2:8)." Pages 62-70 in *The Thessalonian Correspondence.* Edited by Raymond F. Collins. Leuven: Leuven University Press, 1990.

Goldstein, Jonathan A. *The Letters of Demosthenes.* New York: Columbia University Press, 1968.

Goodspeed, Edgar J. *An Introduction to the New Testament.* Chicago: University of Chicago Press, 1937.

Greene, John T. *The Role of the Messenger and Message in the Ancient Near East.* Atlanta: Scholars Press, 1989.

Greenwood, David. "The Lord is the Spirit: Some Considerations of 2 Cor. 3:17." *Catholic Biblical Quarterly* 34 (1972): 467-72.

Hafemann, Scott J. *Suffering and Ministry in the Spirit: Paul's Defense of His Ministry in II Corinthians 2:14–3:3.* Grand Rapids: Eerdmans, 1990.

Hall, Robert G. "The Rhetorical Outline of Galatians: A Reconsideration." *Journal of Biblical Literature* 106 (1987): 277-87.

Harrington, D. J. "Paul and Collaborative Ministry." *New Theological Review* 3 (1990): 62-71.

Hartman, L. "On Reading Others' Letters." *Harvard Theological Review* 79 (1986): 137-46.

Harrisville, Roy A. *I Corinthians.* Augsburg Commentary on the New Testament. Minneapolis: Augsburg, 1987.

Hay, David M., ed. *Pauline Theology Volume II: 1 and 2 Corinthians*. Minneapolis: Fortress, 1993.

Hay, David M., and E. Elizabeth Johnson, eds. *Pauline Theology Volume III: Romans*. Minneapolis: Fortress, 1995.

Hays, Richard B. "Crucified with Christ: A Synthesis of the Theology of 1 and 2 Thessalonians, Philemon, Philippians, and Galatians." Pages 227-46 in *Pauline Theology Volume I: Thessalonians, Philippians, Galatians, Philemon*. Edited by Jouette M. Bassler. Minneapolis: Fortress, 1991.

————. *Echoes of Scripture in the Letters of Paul*. New Haven: Yale University Press, 1989.

————. *First Corinthians*. Louisville: John Knox, 1997.

Hendrickson, G. L. "Ancient Reading." *Classical Journal* 25 (1929-30): 182-84.

Hester, James D. "The Use and Influence of Rhetoric in Galatians 2:1-14." *Theologische Zeitschrift* 42 (1986): 386-408.

Hofmann, Karl-Martin. *Philema hagion*. Gütersloh, 1938.

Holladay, Carl R. "1 Corinthians 13: Paul as Apostolic Paradigm." Pages 80-98 in *Greeks, Romans, and Christians: Essays in Honor of Abraham J. Malherbe*. Edited by David L. Balch, Everett Ferguson, and Wayne A. Meeks. Minneapolis: Fortress, 1990.

Holladay, William L. *Jeremiah 2: A Commentary on the Book of the Prophet Jeremiah, Chapters 26–51*. Hermeneia. Philadelphia: Fortress, 1989.

Hooker, Morna D. *A Preface to Paul*. New York: Oxford University Press, 1980.

————. "Beyond the Things That Are Written? St. Paul's Use of Scripture." *New Testament Studies* 27 (1981): 295-309.

Horgan, Maurya P., and Paul J. Kobelski, eds. *To Touch the Text: Biblical and Related Studies in Honor of Joseph A. Fitzmyer, S.J.* New York: Crossroad Publishing, 1989.

Hughes, Frank Witt. *Early Christian Rhetoric and 2 Thessalonians*. Journal for the Study of the New Testament Supplement Series 30. Sheffield: JSOT Press, 1989.

Hultgren, Arland J. "The Self-Definition of Paul and His Communities." *Svensk exegetisk årsbok* 56 (1991): 78-100.

Jeremias, Joachim. "Paarweise Entsendung im Neuen Testament." Pages 136-44 in *New Testament Essays: Studies in Memory of Thomas Walter Manson*. Edited by A. J. B. Higgins. Manchester: Manchester University Press, 1959.

Jervell, J., and Wayne A. Meeks, eds. *God's Christ and His People: Studies in Honor of Nils Alstrup Dahl*. Oslo: Universitetsforlaget, 1977.

Jervis, L. Ann. *The Purpose of Romans: A Comparative Letter Structure Investigation*. Journal for the Study of the New Testament Supplement Series 55. Sheffield: JSOT Press, 1991.

————. "'But I Want You to Know . . .': Paul's Midrashic Intertextual Response to the Corinthian Worshipers (1 Cor 11:2-16)." *Journal of Biblical Literature* 112 (1993): 231-46.

Jewett, Robert. "Ecumenical Theology for the Sake of Mission: Romans 1:1-17 + 15:14-16:24." Pages 89-108 in *Pauline Theology Volume III: Romans*. Edited by David M. Hay and E. Elizabeth Johnson. Minneapolis: Fortress, 1995.

————. "Romans as an Ambassadorial Letter." *Interpretation* 36 (1982): 5-20.

————. *The Thessalonian Correspondence: Pauline Rhetoric and Millennial Piety*. Philadelphia: Fortress, 1986.

Johnson, Allan Chester, Paul Robinson Coleman-Norton, and Frank Card Bourne. *Ancient Roman Statutes: A Translation with Introduction, Commentary, Glossary, and Index*. Austin: University of Texas Press, 1961.

Johnson, Aubrey Rodway. *The One and the Many in the Israelite Conception of God*. Cardiff: University of Wales Press, 1961.

Juel, Donald H. *1 Thessalonians*. Augsburg Commentary on the New Testament. Minneapolis: Augsburg, 1985.

Karlsson, Gustav. "Formelhaftes in Paulusbriefen?" *Eranos* 54 (1956): 138-41.

Keck, Leander E. *Paul and His Letters*. Proclamation Commentaries. Philadelphia: Fortress, 1979.

————. "What Makes Romans Tick?" Pages 3-29 in *Pauline Theology Volume III: Romans*. Edited by David M. Hay and E. Elizabeth Johnson. Minneapolis: Fortress, 1995.

Kennedy, George A. *Classical Rhetoric and Its Christian and Secular Tradition from Ancient to Modern Times*. Chapel Hill: North Carolina University Press, 1980.

————. *New Testament Interpretation through Rhetorical Criticism*. Chapel Hill: University of North Carolina Press, 1984.

Kim, Chan-Hie, and John L. White. *Letters from the Papyri: A Study Collection*. Consultation on Ancient Epistolography, SBL Epistolography Seminar, 1974.

————. *Form and Structure of the Familiar Greek Letter of Recommendation*. Society of Biblical Literature Dissertation Series 4. Missoula, MT: University of Montana Printing Department, 1972.

Koenig, John. *Philippians, Philemon*. Augsburg Commentary on the New Testament. Minneapolis: Augsburg, 1985.

Koperski, Veronica. "Feminist Concerns and the Authorial Readers in Philippians." *Louvain Studies* 17 (1992): 269-92.

Koskenniemi, Heikki. *Studien zur Idee und Phraseologie des griechischen Briefes bis 400 n. Chr.* Helsinki: Annales Academiae Fennicae, 1956.

Kuck, D. "Paul and Pastoral Ambition: A Reflection on 1 Corinthians 3-4." *Currents in Theology & Mission* 19 (1992): 174-83.

Lietzmann, Hans, and Werner Georg Kümmel. *An die Korinther I II*. Tübingen: Mohr/Siebeck, 1949.

Lieu, Judith M. "'Grace to You and Peace': The Apostolic Greeting." *Bulletin of the John Rylands University Library of Manchester* 86 (1985): 161-78.

Lightfoot, J. B. *The Epistle of St. Paul to the Galatians.* London, 1890; Grand Rapids: Zondervan, 1954.

Lodge, J. G. "The Apostle's Appeal and Readers' Response: 2 Corinthians 8 and 9." *Chicago Studies* 30 (1991): 59-75.

Lohse, Eduard. *Colossians and Philemon.* Hermeneia. Philadelphia: Fortress, 1971.

Lyons, George. *Pauline Autobiography: Toward a New Understanding.* Society of Biblical Literature Dissertation Series 73. Atlanta: Scholars Press, 1985.

McGuire, Martin R. P. "Letters and Letter Carriers in Christian Antiquity." *Classical World* 53 (1960): 148-53, 184-85, 199-200.

Mack, Burton L., and Vernon K. Robbins. *Patterns of Persuasion in the Gospels.* Sonoma, CA: Polebridge, 1989.

Malherbe, Abraham J. *Ancient Epistolary Theorists.* Society of Biblical Literature Sources for Biblical Study 19. Atlanta: Scholars Press, 1988.

———. *Paul and the Popular Philosophers.* Philadelphia: Fortress, 1989.

———. *Social Aspects of Early Christianity.* Philadelphia: Fortress, 1983.

———. "Did the Thessalonians Write to Paul?" Pages 246-57 in *The Conversation Continues: Studies in Paul and John in Honor of Louis Martyn.* Edited by Robert T. Fortna and Beverly R. Gaventa. Nashville: Abingdon, 1990.

———. *Paul and the Thessalonians: The Philosophic Tradition of Pastoral Care.* Philadelphia: Fortress, 1987.

———. *The Cynic Epistles.* Society of Biblical Literature Sources for Biblical Studies 12. Atlanta: Scholars Press, 1977.

Mantel, Hugo. *Studies in the History of the Sanhedrin.* Cambridge, MA: Harvard University Press, 1961.

Martin, Troy. "Apostasy to Paganism: The Rhetorical Stasis of the Galatian Controversy." *Journal of Biblical Literature* 114 (1995): 437-61.

Mayer, Bernhard. "Paulus als Vermittler zwischen Epaphroditus und der Gemeinde von Philippi, Bemerkungen zu Phil 2,25-30." *Biblische Zeitschrift* 31 (1987): 167-88.

Meeks, Wayne A. *The First Urban Christians: The Social World of the Apostle Paul.* New Haven: Yale University Press, 1983.

———. "The Man from Heaven in Paul's Letter to the Philippians." Pages 329-36 in *The Future of Early Christianity: Essays in Honor of Helmut Koester.* Edited by Birger A. Pearson. Minneapolis: Fortress, 1991.

Meier, Samuel A. *The Messenger in the Ancient Semitic World.* Harvard Semitic Monographs 45. Atlanta: Scholars Press, 1988.

Merklein, Helmut. "Der Theologe als Prophet: zur Funktion prophetischen Redens im theologischen Diskurs des Paulus." *New Testament Studies* 38 (1992): 402-29.

Millar, Fergus. "Emperors at Work." *Journal of Roman Studies* 57 (1967): 9-19.

Milligan, George. *Here and There among the Papyri.* London: Hodder & Stoughton, 1922.

Mitchell, Margaret M. "New Testament Envoys in the Context of Greco-Roman Diplomatic and Epistolary Conventions: The Example of Timothy and Titus." *Journal of Biblical Literature* III (1992): 641-62.

——. *Paul and the Rhetoric of Reconciliation: An Exegetical Investigation of the Language and Composition of I Corinthians.* Hermeneutische Untersuchungen zur Theologie 28. Tübingen: Mohr/Siebeck, 1991; Louisville: Westminster/John Knox, 1992.

——. "Concerning *PERI DE* in I Corinthians." *Novum Testamentum* 31 (1989): 229-56.

Moore, A. L. *The Parousia in the New Testament.* Novum Testamentum Supplement 13. Leiden: E. J. Brill, 1966.

Mullins, Terence Y. "Greeting as a New Testament Form." *Journal of Biblical Literature* 87 (1968): 418-26.

——. "Petition as a Literary Form." *Novum Testamentum* 5 (1962): 46-54.

Murphy-O'Connor, Jerome. "Co-Authorship in the Corinthian Correspondence." *Revue Biblique* 100 (1993): 562-79.

——. *Paul the Letter-Writer: His World, His Options, His Skills.* Good News Studies 41. Collegeville, MN: Liturgical Press, 1995.

Myers, J. M., O. Reimherr, and H. N. Bream, eds. *Search the Scriptures: New Testament Studies in Honor of Raymond T. Stamm.* Leiden: Brill, 1969.

Neusner, Jacob. *A Life of Rabban Yohanan ben Zakkai ca. I-80 C.E.* Leiden: E. J. Brill, 1962.

Nickle, Keith F. *The Collection: A Study in Paul's Strategy.* Studies in Biblical Theology 48. Naperville, IL: Allenson, 1966.

O'Brien, Peter Thomas. *Introductory Thanksgivings in the Letters of Paul.* Novum Testamentum Supplement 49. Leiden: E. J. Brill, 1977.

Olson, Stanley N. "Epistolary Uses of Expressions of Self-Confidence." *Journal of Biblical Literature* 103 (1984): 585-97.

Orr, William F., and James Arthur Walther. *I Corinthians: A New Translation.* The Anchor Bible. Garden City, NY: Doubleday, 1976.

Pardee, Dennis. "An Overview of Ancient Hebrew Epistolography." *Journal of Biblical Literature* 97 (1978): 321-46.

Pearson, Birger A., ed. *The Future of Early Christianity: Essays in Honor of Helmut Koester.* Minneapolis: Fortress, 1991.

Perkins, Pheme. "Philippians: Theology for the Heavenly Politeuma." Pages 89-104 in *Pauline Theology Volume I: Thessalonians, Philippians, Galatians, Philemon.* Edited by Jouette M. Bassler. Minneapolis: Fortress, 1991.

Perry, A. M. "Epistolary Form in Paul." *Crozer Quarterly* 26 (1949): 48-53.

Peterman, G. W. *Paul's Gift from Philippi: Conventions of Gift-Exchange and Christian Giving.* Society for New Testament Studies Monograph Series 92. Cambridge: Cambridge University Press, 1997.

Petersen, Norman R. *Rediscovering Paul: Philemon and the Sociology of Paul's Narrative World.* Philadelphia: Fortress, 1985.

———. "On the Ending(s) of Paul's Letter to Rome." Pages 337-47 in *The Future of Early Christianity: Essays in Honor of Helmut Koester.* Edited by Birger A. Pearson. Minneapolis: Fortress, 1991.

Plevnik, Joseph. "Pauline Presuppositions." Pages 50-61 in *The Thessalonian Correspondence.* Edited by Raymond F. Collins. Leuven: Leuven University Press/Peeters, 1990.

Porter, S. E., and T. H. Olbricht, eds. *Rhetoric and the New Testament: Essays from the 1992 Heidelberg Conference.* Journal for the Study of the New Testament Supplement Series 90. Sheffield: JSOT Press, 1993.

Preisigke, Friedrich. "Die ptolemaische Staatspost." *Klio* 7 (1907): 241-77.

Probst, Hermann. *Paulus und der Brief: Die Rhetorik des antiken Briefes als Form der paulinischen Korintherkorrespondenz.* Wissenschaftliche Untersuchungen zum Neuen Testament 2:45. Tübingen: Mohr/Siebeck, 1991.

Ramsey, William M. *A Historical Commentary on St. Paul's Epistle to the Galatians.* New York, 1900; Grand Rapids: Baker, 1965.

Reed, Jeffrey T. "Philippians 3:1 and the Epistolary Hesitation Formulas: The Literary Integrity of Philippians Again." *Journal of Biblical Literature* 115 (1990): 63-90.

Richards, E. Randolf. *The Secretary in the Letters of Paul.* Wissenschaftliche Unterschungen zum Neuen Testament 2:42. Tübingen: Mohr/Siebeck, 1991.

Roller, Otto. *Das Formular der paulinischen Briefe: Ein Beitrag zur Lehre von antike Briefen.* Stuttgart: Kohlhammer, 1933.

Russel, Ronald. "Pauline Letter Structure in Philippians." *Journal of the Evangelical Theological Society* 25 (1982): 295-306.

Sampley, J. Paul. "Paul, His Opponents in 2 Corinthians 10-13, and the Rhetorical Handbooks." Pages 162-77 in *The Social World of Formative Christianity and Judaism in Tribute to Howard Clark Kee.* Edited by Jacob Neusner, Ernest S. Frerichs, Peter Borgen, and Richard Horsley. Philadelphia: Fortress, 1988.

———. "Romans in a Different Light." Pages 109-29 in *Pauline Theology Volume III: Romans.* Edited by David M. Hay and E. Elizabeth Johnson. Minneapolis: Fortress, 1995.

Sandnes, Karl Olav. *Paul — One of the Prophets? A Contribution to the Apostle's Self-Understanding.* Wissenschaftliche Untersuchungen zum Neuen Testament 2:43. Tübingen: Mohr/Siebeck, 1991.

Schafer, K. *Gemeinde als Bruderschaft: Ein Beitrag zum Kirchenstandnis des Paulus.* Frankfurt: Lang, 1989.

Schnider, Franz, and Werner Stenger. *Studien zum neutestamentlichen Briefformular.* New Testament Tools and Studies 11. Leiden: E. J. Brill, 1987.

Schubert, Paul. "Form and Function of the Pauline Letters." *Journal of Religion* 19 (1939): 365-77.

———. *Form and Function of the Pauline Thanksgivings.* Berlin: Töpelmann, 1939.

———. "Urgent Tasks for New Testament Research." Pages 209-28 in *The Study of the Bible Today and Tomorrow.* Edited by Harold R. Willoughby. Chicago: Chicago University Press, 1947.

Schütz, John Howard. *Paul and the Anatomy of Apostolic Authority.* Society for New Testament Studies Monograph Series 26. Cambridge: Cambridge University Press, 1975.

Scott, James M. "Paul's Use of Deuteronomic Tradition." *Journal of Biblical Literature* (1993): 645-65.

Segal, Alan F. *Paul the Convert: The Apostolate and Apostasy of Saul the Pharisee.* New Haven: Yale University Press, 1990.

Sherk, Robert K. *Roman Documents from the Greek East: Senatus Consulta and Epistulae to the Age of Augustus.* Baltimore: Johns Hopkins Press, 1969.

Skeat, T. C. "Did Paul Write to 'Bishops and Deacons' at Philippi? A Note on Philippians 1:1." *Novum Testamentum* 37 (1995): 12-13.

Smit, Joop. "The Letter of Paul to the Galatians: A Deliberative Speech." *New Testament Studies* 35 (1989): 1-26.

Spallek, A. J. "The Origin and Meaning of *Euangelion* in the Pauline Corpus." *Concordia Theological Quarterly* 57 (1993): 177-90.

Stendahl, Krister. *Final Account: Paul's Letter to the Romans.* Minneapolis: Fortress, 1995.

———. *Meanings: The Bible as Document and Guide.* Philadelphia: Fortress, 1984.

Stirewalt, M. Luther Jr. "The Form and Function of the Greek Letter-Essay." Pages 147-71 in *The Romans Debate.* Revised and expanded edition. Edited by Karl P. Donfried. Peabody, MA: Hendrickson, 1991.

———. "Paul's Evaluation of Letter-Writing." Pages 179-96 in *Search the Scriptures: New Testament Studies in Honor of Raymond T. Stamm.* Edited by J. M. Meyers, O. Reimherr, and H. N. Bream. Leiden: E. J. Brill, 1969.

———. *Studies in Ancient Greek Epistolography.* Society of Biblical Literature Resources for Biblical Study 27. Atlanta: Scholars Press, 1993.

Stockhausen, Carol Kern. *Letters in the Pauline Tradition: Ephesians, Colossians, I Timothy, II Timothy and Titus.* Wilmington, DE: Liturgical Press, 1989.

———. *Moses' Veil and the Glory of the New Covenant: The Exegetical Substructure of II Cor. 3,1–4,6.* Analecta Biblica 116. Rome: Editrice Pontificio Instituto Biblico, 1989.

Stone, Michael E. *Jewish Writings of the Second Temple Period: Apocrypha, Pseudepig-rapha, Qumran, Sectarian Writings, Philo, Josephus.* Assen: Van Gorcum; Phil-adelphia: Fortress, 1984.

Stowers, Stanley K. "Friends and Enemies in the Politics of Heaven: Reading Theology in Philippians." Pages 105-21 in *Pauline Theology Volume I: Thessalonians, Philippians, Galatians, Philemon.* Edited by Jouette M. Bassler. Minneapolis: Fortress, 1991.

———. *Letter Writing in Greco-Roman Antiquity.* Philadelphia: Westminster, 1986.

———. "*Peri men gar* and the Integrity of 2 Cor. 8 and 9." *Novum Testamentum* 32 (1990): 340-48.

———. *A Reading of Romans.* New Haven and London: Yale University Press, 1994.

———. "Social Typification and the Classification of Ancient Letters." Pages 78-90 in *The Social World of Formative Christianity and Judaism in Tribute to Howard Clark Kee.* Edited by Jacob Neusner et al. Philadelphia: Fortress, 1988.

Taatz, Irene. *Frühjüdische Briefe: Die paulinische Briefe im Rahmen der offiziellen religiösen Briefe des Frühjudentums.* Novum Testamentum et Orbis Antiquis 16. Freiburg: Universitätsverlag; Göttingen: Vandenhoeck and Ruprecht, 1991.

Theissen, Gerd. *The Social Setting of Pauline Christianity: Essays on Corinth.* Phila-delphia: Fortress, 1982.

Thraede, Klaus. *Grundzüge griechisch-römischer Brieftopik.* Zetemata 48. München: C. H. Beck, 1970.

Tuckett, C. M. "Synoptic Tradition in 1 Thessalonians?" Pages 160-82 in *The Thessalonian Correspondence.* Edited by Raymond F. Collins. Leuven: Leuven University Press/Peeters, 1990.

Vanhoye, Albert, ed. *L'Apotre Paul: Personalite, style et conception du ministere.* Bibliotheca ephemeridum theologicarum lovaniensium 73. Leuven: Leuven University Press, 1986.

———. "La composition de 1 Thessaloniens." Pages 73-86 in *The Thessalonian Correspondence.* Edited by Raymond F. Collins. Leuven: Leuven University Press, 1990.

Venetz, Hermann-Josef. "Stephanas, Fortunatus, Achaikus, Epaphroditus, Epaphras, Onesimus and Co. Die Frage nach den Gemeindevertretern und Gemeindegesandten in den paulinischen Gemeinden." Pages 13-38 in *Peregrina Couriositas: Eine Reise durch den orbis antiquus.* Edited by Andreas Kessler, Thomas Ricklin, & Gregor Wurst. Freiburg, Schweiz: Universitätsverlag; Göttingen: Vandenhoeck and Ruprecht, 1994.

Verbrugge, Verlyn Davis. *The Collection and Paul's Leadership of the Church in Cor-inth.* Ann Arbor: University of Michigan Press, 1988.

———. *Paul's Style of Church Leadership Illustrated by His Instructions to the Corinthians on the Collection.* San Francisco: Mellen Research University Press, 1992.

———. "Rhetorical Criticism of the Pauline Epistles Since 1975." *Currents in Research: Biblical Studies* 3 (1995): 219-48.

Vouga, François. "Zur rhetorischen Gattung des Galaterbriefes." *Zeitschrift für die neutestamentliche Wissenschaft und die Kunde der alteren Kirche* 79 (1988): 291-92.

Walter, Nikolaus. "Paul and the Early Christian Jesus-Tradition." Pages 51-80 in *Paul and Jesus: Collected Essays.* Edited by A. J. M. Wedderburn. Journal for the Study of the New Testament Supplement Series 37. Sheffield: JSOT Press, 1989.

Wanamaker, C. A. "Christ as Divine Agent in Paul." *Scottish Journal of Theology* 39 (1986): 517-28.

Watson, Duane F. "1 Corinthians 10:23–11:1 in the Light of Greco-Roman Rhetoric: The Role of Rhetorical Questions." *Journal of Biblical Literature* 108 (1989): 301-18.

———. "A Rhetorical Analysis of Philippians and Its Implication for the Unity Question." *Novum Testamentum* 30 (1988): 57-88.

———. "Rhetorical Criticism of the Pauline Epistles Since 1975." *Currents in Research: Biblical Studies* 3 (1995): 219-48.

Wedderburn, A. J. M., ed. *Paul and Jesus: Collected Essays.* Journal for the Study of the New Testament Supplement Series 37. Sheffield: JSOT Press, 1989.

Wegener, Mark I. "Philippians 2:6-11 — Paul's (Revised) Hymn to Jesus." *Currents in Theology and Mission* 25 (1998): 506-17.

Welborn, L. L. "On the Discord in Corinth: 1 Corinthians 1–4 and Ancient Politics." *Journal of Biblical Literature* 106 (1987): 85-111.

Welles, C. Bradford. *Royal Correspondence in the Hellenistic Period: A Study in Greek Epistolography.* New Haven: Yale University Press, 1934. Reprint, Chicago: Ares, 1974.

White, John L. *The Apostle of God: Paul and the Promise of Abraham.* Peabody, MA: Hendrickson, 1999.

———. "Apostolic Mission and Apostolic Message: Congruence in Paul's Epistolary Rhetoric, Structure and Imagery." Pages 145-62 in *Origins and Method: Toward a New Understanding of Judaism and Christianity: Essays in Honor of John C. Hurd.* Edited by Bradley H. McLean. Sheffield: JSOT Press, 1993.

———. *The Form and Function of the Body of the Greek Letter: A Study of the Letter-Body in the Non-Literary Papyri and in Paul the Apostle.* Society of Biblical Literature Dissertation Series 2. Missoula, MT: University of Montana Printing Department, 1972.

———. *The Form and Structure of the Official Petition: A Study in Greek Epis-

tolography. Society of Biblical Literature Dissertation Series 5. Missoula, MT: Scholars Press, 1972.

———. *Light from Ancient Letters*. Philadelphia: Fortress, 1986.

———. "Saint Paul and the Apostolic Letter Tradition." *Catholic Biblical Quarterly* 45 (1983): 433-44.

———. "The Greek Documentary Tradition Third Century B.C.E. to Third Century C.E." Pages 89-106 in *Studies in Ancient Letter Writing*. Edited by John L. White. Semeia 22. Chico, CA: Scholars Press, 1982.

White, L. Michael. "Morality between Two Worlds: A Paradigm of Friendship in Philippians." Pages 201-15 in *Greeks, Romans, and Christians: Essays in Honor of Abraham J. Malherbe*. Edited by David L. Balch, Everett Ferguson, and Wayne A. Meeks. Minneapolis: Fortress, 1990.

Wilder, Amos N. *The Language of the Gospel: Early Christian Rhetoric*. New York: Harper and Row, 1964.

Wilson, Andrew. "The Pragmatics of Politeness and Pauline Epistolography: A Case Study of the Letter to Philemon." *Journal for the Study of the New Testament* 48 (1992): 107-19.

Winter, S. B. C. "Methodological Observations on a New Interpretation of Paul's Letter to Philemon." *Union Seminary Quarterly Review* 39 (1984): 203-12.

Wuellner, Wilhelm. "Greek Rhetoric and Pauline Argumentation." Pages 177-88 in *Early Christian Literature and the Classical Tradition: An R. M. Grant Festschrift*. Edited by William R. Schoedel and Robert L. Wilken. Paris: Éditions Beauchesne, 1979.

———. The Argumentive Structure of 1 Thessalonians as Paradoxical Encomium." Pages 117-36 in *The Thessalonian Correspondence*. Edited by Raymond F. Collins. Leuven: Leuven University Press/Peeters, 1990.

———. "Paul's Rhetoric of Argumentation in Romans: An Alternative to the Donfried-Karris Debate." Pages 144-52 in *The Romans Debate*. Edited by Karl P. Donfried. Peabody, MA: Hendrickson, 1991.

———. "Where Is Rhetorical Criticism Taking Us?" *Catholic Biblical Quarterly* 49 (1987): 448-63.

Young, Frances M., and David F. Ford. *Meaning and Truth in 2 Corinthians*. Grand Rapids: Eerdmans, 1988.

Index of Scripture References

OLD TESTAMENT		APOCRYPHA		NEW TESTAMENT	
				Mark	115
Deuteronomy		**2 Baruch**			
19:15	44	78–86	8n.36	**Acts**	19
				9:1-2	19
				15	44, 110n.86
1 Kings		**1 Maccabees**		15:22-23	12n.47
21:8	45n.41	7:1	45n.42	15:22ff.	102
		11:30	45n.41	15:22-29	44, 124n.17
		11:57	8n.35	15:22-35	19, 106
2 Kings		12:6	40	15:23	40, 41n.35,
19:1	45n.41	13:36	45n.41		99n.72
19:8-14	14n.53	14:16	45n.42	15:27	7n.31
		14:16ff.	8n.35	15:30-32	7
		14:20b	79n.31	17	58
Ezra		14:20b-23	32	17:1-9	58
4:17-24	14n.53	15:2b	45n.41	18:27	18n.73
		15:16-21	47n.48	23:25-30	18n.73
				28:21	18n.73, 100n.73
Isaiah					
37:8-14	14n.53	**2 Maccabees**		**Romans**	9, 14, 37, 46,
		1:1	99n.72		57, 58, 88, 94,
Jeremiah		9:19-27	47n.48		107-12, 117
29:1	43, 45n.41			1:8	123n.15
29:4	45n.41			1:13	21n.74
29:23b	43	**3 Maccabees**		1:16–11:36	112
29:24-25	45n.41	3:12	45n.42, 79n.31	2:1-4	111
36:4-8	8n.37	7:1	79n.31		